THE MICROECONOMIC THEORY

Dedicated to

My

Students

Preface:

To author the book is not an easy task. It requires hardship, continuous efforts, active dynamism & the innovative approach. The present edition on "The Microeconomic Theory" is the outcome of such dynamism & is an attempt to make the contents easily understandable & digestible to the learners in the related field. In this age of information, communication, technology & globalization it the competitive skill & strength that rules & governs the world. Such competitive skills are to be cultivated among the young minds. This is possible when knowledge is acquired, facts are collected & self analysis of the facts is done. So the young minds need to cultivate the skills & the knowledge by the continuous & dynamic approach. In this edition, the focus is on the micro aspects of the economy as the consumer demand, consumer equilibrium, the supply side, the producer equilibrium, markets, factor pricing & finally the welfare economics. I hope the present edition will be helpful to the learners in the related fields as economics, commerce, business & other competitive exams. I am very indebtful to all to those who helped me by their expert advice to complete the present edition.

The author

Acknowledgement:

This book on "The Microeconomic Theory" is the outcome of expert advices, suggestions & the encouragement from the parents, the colleagues & the senior faculty at College as well the society & above intuition from the spiritual philosophy. I express my thanks & gratitude to my parents, family who gave me time to author this book.

My thanks to my College colleagues & seniors for their valuable suggestions. My special thanks to Prof. Depanker Sen, HoD, and Deptt. of Economics, University of Jammu for his moral support from time to time. Thanks to Dr. Jasbir Singh, Reader & Prof. Subash for their valuable suggestions.

My thanks go to Dr. P.S.Bisht, Reader, and Deptt. Of Economic, DSB Campus, Komoun University, Nainital for guiding me from time to time.Thanks to the Library staff at Central Library, University of Jammu who helped me to access the required material.

Last but not least thanks to the publishers for speedy publication of this edition.

Surinder Singh Parihar

Sr. Asstt. Prof. of Economics

GDC Bhaderwah J & K.

Contents:

Unit 4

Factor Pricing(122-150)

:Distribution-Concept:Marginal productivity theory, wages-Modern theory of wages, Wage differentials,Rent-concepts,Ricardian theory of rent, Profits-Innovation & Dynamic theory,Interst :Classical & Keynesian Theory

Unit 5

Welfare Economics(151-162)

Concept, the classical welfare economics, the Paretian welfare & marginal conditions, the compensation principle, Scitovsky Paradox & its resolve, new welfare economics, role of the value judgments .

(Note: Semester 1st students affiliated to Jammu University for three year degree courses have to skip the 5th unit which has been deleted from the current syllabus.)

UNIT 1ST

ECONOMICS:-An Introduction

Tits-bits:

Economics: The science of managing limited resources to meet unlimited wants.

Microeconomics: When we study the part of economy.

Macroeconomics: When we study the economy as a whole.

Economic activity: the activity which is related to income or money as to produce, to consume, to spend, to invest etc.

Economic system: The system in which economic activities are carried out also known as the economy.

Market economy: The economy where the market forces of supply & demand play the major role automatically.

Command economy: The market where the government plays the major role in the economy.

Mixed economy: The market where both the government & the private sector co-exist.

Positive economics: The branch of economics which studies what is, why is how is.

Normative economics: The branch of economics which studies what should be, why should be & how should be.

Wealth: It means the means of production includes money, materials, machinery, property etc.

Welfare: It means happiness of the society which possible when goods & services are available at reasonable rates.

Economic problem: The basic problem of the economics is the problem of choice which is the result of scarcity.

Scarcity: The situation when the demand exceeds the supply.

Choice: The problem of selection among various alternatives. It is the basic problem of the economics.

Assumptions: The conditions or suppositions on which the facts are validated.

Utility: The want satisfying power of the goods & services is called utility.

Cardinal utility: When the utility is measurable in quantitative terms, the concept is called cardinal.

Ordinal Utility: Actually utility is not measurable in quantitative terms but rankable as more or less, higher or lower level, so utility is known as ordinal that is orderable or rankable.

Total Utility (TU): The total satisfaction from the units of a good consumed.

Marginal Utility (MU): The additional satisfaction from the additional unit of a good consumed.

Consumer`s Equilibrium Point: The situation when the consumer gets maximum satisfaction.

Diminishing MU: As the good increases with the consumer, the marginal utility goes on diminishing.

Marginal Rate of Substitution (MRS):-The rate at which one good is exchanged for another.

Substitute Goods: Those goods which can be substituted for each other, e.g. tea for coffee, lux soap for dettol soap etc.

Complementary Goods: Those goods which have joint demand, e.g. pen & ink, car & petrol etc.

Elasticity of demand: The response of change in demand to the change in price, income or prices of the related goods.

Consumer`s Surplus: The extra benefit to the that appears and is calculated as the willingness to pay minus actual price in the market.

What is Economics: An Introduction:-

Introduction:-The word economics has been derived from two Greek words Oikos (house hold) & Nemein (management) thus economics mean household management. Therefore the economics is the science of managing the limited resources to meet the unlimited wants at home, local, regional, national or international level.

Prior to 1776,the French writers called Physicrates stressed the need for agriculture to make the economy rich, the mercantilists writers advocated to collect more gold & silver to make the country rich in 16th century but Adam Smith who was born in 1723 at a village Kirkaldy,Scotland compiled all the previous thought & added his own & got published his great work entitled`` An Enquiry into the nature & causes of the Wealth of Nations" in 1776 for which he got the status of the Father of the Economics. According to Prof L.H.Haney same work was done by Prof. Quesnay in France but because of British greater say then the title of fatherhood was given to Sir Adam Smith. So the Sir Smith is known the father of the modern political economy.

Smith`s title of the book became the definition of economics i.e. economics is an enquiry into the nature & causes of the wealth of nations & labour & capital are the sources of all wealth. This definition is known as the wealth definition of economics.

Later in 1890 Sir Alfred Marshall added that economics studies wealth on the one side & material welfare of the mankind on the other side.i.e availability of material goods. Sir Marshall ignored immaterial goods or services as services by doctors, teachers, lawyers, bankers etc

However in 1932 Lionel Robbins went further near to reality & said economics studies human behavior as a relationship between the unlimited wants (ends) & limited resources (means) which have alternative uses. But he was criticized for ignoring the affluence (richness) of some countries as the

USA & the UK.Still this definition is universally acceptable because of the scarcity & thus the problem of choice, so economic is the science of scarcity & thus the basic problem is the problem of the choice.

In 1950s Prof. Samuelson focused on the economic growth i.e. economics studies the economic growth which covers production consumption, exchange, distribution, investment etc.

Nature & Scope of Economics:

Nature means weather the economics is science or an art, further weather it is the positive science or the normative science.

As Science: Like science the economics is the body of knowledge, some laws of economics are universal.e.g. the law of diminishing returns, the experiments are conducted in the open field, thus to some extent it can be treated as science but not an exact science better we call it a social science because its laws are not universal, close laboratory experiments are not possible.

AS a positive science:-The positive science studies what is, how is why i.e. given facts. Likewise Economics also studies the given facts, e.g. the poverty is high in India, the unemployment is high etc.Thus economics is a positive science.

As a normative science:-The normative science studies what should be, how should be & why should be,i.e it suggests, prescribes. Likewise economics also studies normative aspects as the poverty, unemployment; inequities should be reduced in India.

Thus economics is both a positive & a normative science.

AS an Art:-An art is practice, action. It is practical use of the knowledge. As the economics provides us tools & policies for the practical use in the economy, so economics can be treated as an art.

Conclusion:-Thus it can be concluded that the economics is both science & an art also it is both a positive & a normative science.

Scope:-The scope implies the field or area or the subject or its boundary. Thus economics covers following areas:

1. **Economic Activities**: All the activities which have relation with money or income are called the economic activities.e.g. Production (creation of utility), consumption (use of utility), distribution, exchange etc.
2. **Micro & Macroeconomic activities**:-Micro economics means when we consider the part of the economy & macro economics means when we consider the whole economy .e.g. J & K is micro & India is a macro concept the Indian economy.

Points	Microeconomics	Macroeconomic

		s
1.Definition	Microeconomics studies the part of the economy	Macroeconomics studies the whole economy.
2.Subject Matter	It studies indidual units, firms, markets e.g. individual firm, individual market demand etc.	It studies aggregates as National income, general price level, Money supply, growth & development etc
3.Assumptios	It assumes ceteri paribus (other things remaining the same.)	It keeps all sectors into consideration even as per model need uses ceteris paribus.
4.Interdependence	Micro depends on macro for aggregates.	Micro depends on macro for individual units.
5.Examples	Jammu & Kashmir,Himachal Pradesh, Kerala	India, China

3. **The economic systems**:-The economic system is the type of the economy in which the economic activities are performed to earn livelihood. Presently there are the types of the economies:

    a. The Market Economy b.The Command Economy c.The Mixed Economy

Points	Market economy	Command economy	Mixed economy
1.Type	It is the capitalist or the market economy.	It is the socialist economy.	Here both the public & private sectors co-exist.
2.Resouces/Factors of production	The resources remain in the private hands.	The resources remain with the state/govt.	Both with the private & the public sector
3.Pricing system	The economy operates through price mechanism with the automatic working of the demand & the supply forces.	The prices are decided by the government.	In public sector by the govt.
4.Govt. interference	Little or none.	Heavy	Moderate

5.Motive	The system works for the profits only.	For welfare.	The govt. sector for the welfare & the private sector for the profits
5.e.g.	The USA, the UK etc	Poland, Cuba etc	India, Srilanka,Pakistan etc

4. The economic policies:-The economics provide various economic policies such as the fiscal, monetary, trade, price, income, wage policies etc.The fiscal policy is the govt. policy to regulate the behavior of the tax, debt, deficit financing (issuing fresh currency) & the expenditure, the monetary policy regulates the money supply in the economy, the trade policy deals with the exports & the imports.

Utility Analysis:-Utility means want satisfying power of goods & services. It can be categorized as

A.**Crdinal Utility Analysis**   B.**Ordinal Utility Analysis**

A. **Cardinal Utility Analysis**:-Sir Alfred Marshal is associated with cardinal measure of utility, even though utility cannot be measured in numerical terms but can be said as more or less satisfaction.

Meaning of Cardinal Utility:-It means utility can be measured by cardinal numbers as 1, 2, 10, and 20 etc.That is utility is an additive concept & can be expressed in numbers exactly.eg. It can be said how satisfaction is obtained after drinking one glass of juice or milk.

Utility has two aspectst:1-TU i.e. total utility meaning satisfaction from all the units of a good in consideration &2. MU, i.e. marginal utility meaning additional satisfaction from the additional unit of the good consumed.

Assumptions:-The cardinal utility analysis is based on following assumptions:-

1. Utility is cardinal concept, i.e. numerically measurable.

2. Utility is an independent concept, i.e. satisfaction from one good has nothing to do with another good.

3. Marginal utility for money will remain constant.

4. Introspection, i.e. judging other`s mind by one`s own experience.

Explanation:-The utility analysis can be explained with the help of table & diagram as under:- In the table when the consumer comes 1st unit of good ,TU is 10 UTILS(an imaginary unit) ,MU is 10,as the consumer consumes 2nd unit

TU goes to 18,MU declines to 8, so on when he/she consumes 6th unit ,TU becomes maximum,i.e. 30 but MU falls to minimum,i.e. 0 & further when he/she consumes 7th unit ,TU starts declining, MU becomes negative.

Table1.1:-law of Diminishing Marginal Utility(DMU)

Units of Ice cream	TU	MU
1	10	10
2	18	8
3	24	6
4	28	4
5	30	2
6	30	0
7	28	-2

Diagrammatical presentation: :- In the figure1.1, along ox-axis we have taken units of ice cream & along oy-axis TU/MU when the consumer comes 1st unit of good ,TU is 10 UTILS ,MU is 10,as the consumer consumes 2nd unit TU goes to 18,MU declines to 8, so on when he/she consumes 6th unit

,TU becomes maximum,i.e. 30 but MU falls to minimum,i.e. 0 & further when he/she consumes 7th unit ,TU starts declining, MU becomes negative. This explains the law of DMU.

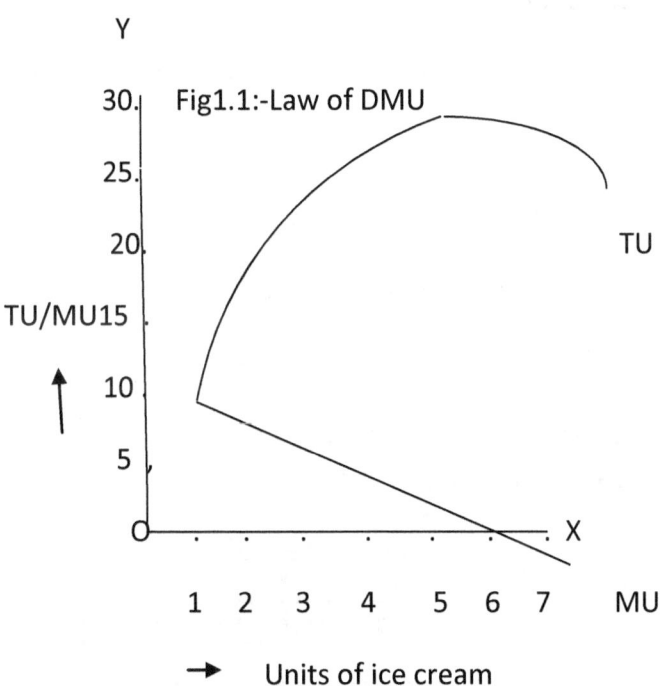

Fig1.1:-Law of DMU

Units of ice cream

Laws of the cardinal utility Analysis:-There are two laws of utility developed by Sir H.H.Gossen, an Austrian economist.

1. **Law of DMU (Gossen's 1st law)**   2.**Law of EMU (Gossen's 2nd law)**

Law of DMU:-According to the law of DMU, as the stock of the good increases with the consumer ,the marginal utility for the same good goes on diminishing, i.e. additional satisfaction from the additional units of a good goes on declining.

Assumptions:-

1. Nature, size & quality of the good should not.

2. The consumption should be continuous.

3. The taste should remain the same.

4. The good should be normal.

5. The consumer should be normal

Explanation:-The law can be explained with the help of a table & diagram as under:-

Table1.2:-Law of DMU

Units of Ice cream	TU	MU
1	10	10
2	18	8
3	24	6
4	28	4
5	30	2
6	30	0
7	28	-2

Diagrammatical presentation:

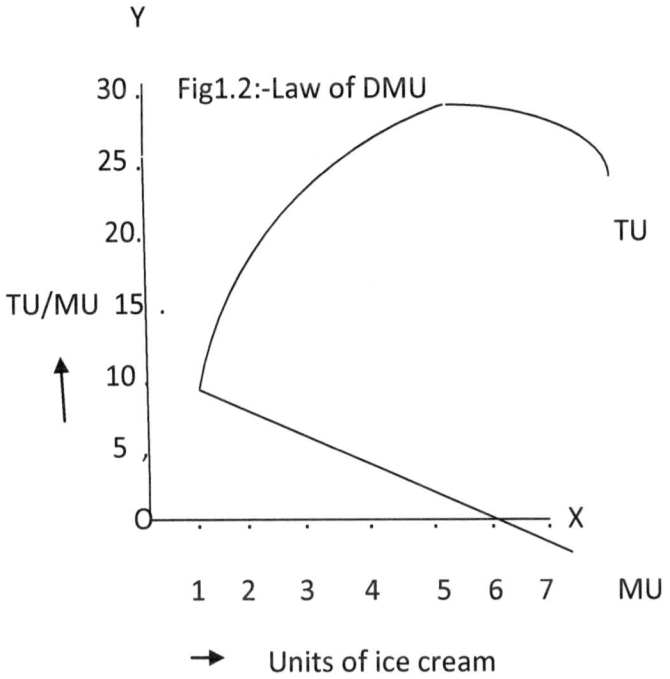

Y

Fig1.2:-Law of DMU

TU

TU/MU

MU

Units of ice cream

2. **Law of Equi-Marginal Utility(EMU)**:-According to the law of EMU, MUm (Marginal utility of money) should be same for all the goods purchased by the consumer, i.e

Mum=MUx/Px=MUy/Py=........=MUn/Pn

Where MU is marginal utility, m is money& x,y...n are goods up to any number n.

Explanation:-The law can be explained with the help of table & diagram as under:

Table1.3:-law of EMU

Units	MUx	MUy	MUx/Px	MUy/Py
1	50	100	5	5

2	40	80	4	4	
3	**30**	**60**	**3**	**3**	Eqbm. point
4	20	40	2	2	
5	10	20	1	1	

Diagrammatical presentation:-

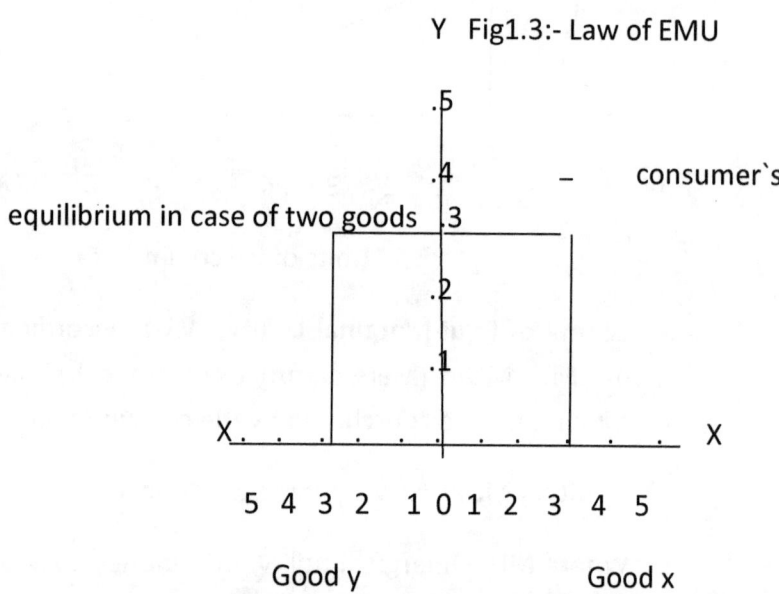

Y   Fig1.3:- Law of EMU

–   consumer`s

equilibrium in case of two goods

5 4 3 2   1 0 1 2 3 4 5

Good y   Good x

2.   **Ordinal   Utility   Analysis/Indifference   curve technique/Hicks-Allen   Approach**:-Indifference   technique was invented by Francis Ysidro Edgeworth in 1881,Pareto 1906, ,Slutsky in 1915 ,finally shaped by Hicks-Allen in 1939.Ordinal concept means   that utility is a rankable, orderable concept not numerically measurable.

Assumptions:- 1. Utility is an ordinal concept. That is it can said as more or less as more happy less happy not as happiness is equal to 10 or 20.

2. MRS is diminishing. The rate at which one good is exchanged for another is called MRS. It is assumed diminishing as the consumer does not want other good to go totally.

3. Consumer is rational in nature. It means consumer can & do make choices. More over he/she wants maximum.

4. Prices, income   given for the consumer. These are assumed to not change during analysis.

5. Ordering is weak. It means consumer can prefer choice A to B or vice versa or remain indifferent to both.

6. Preference is indifference. It means consumer can give equal preference or rank to his /her bundle of goods

7. Preference is complete. It means consumer has capacity to rank & set the preference order.

8.Consistency:It means if consumer says choice A is better than B,& B better than C, then he cannot say C is better than A.

9. Transitivity: It means if A is preferred to B, B to C, then A should be preferred to C.

Indifference Curve & Properties/Features/Characteristics of Indifference Curves

Indifference Curve(IC) :-The curve which shows consumer`s preference schedule for the different combinations of any two goods. This curve gives equal satisfaction to the consumer on all its points indication different combinations of any two goods.

Explanation:-The IC can be explained with the help of a table & diagram as under:-

Table1.4:-Indifference Curve

Combination	Good X	Good Y	MRS
A	1	13	-
B	2	9	4
C	3	6	3
D	4	4	2
E	5	3	1

The table 1.4 shows 1X & 13Y in preference combination A & combination B shows 2X & 9Y & so on as good X is increasing, the quantity of Good Y is decreasing. In this exchange the MRS is decreasing from 4 to 1.

Diagrammatical Presentation:- The figure shows 1X & 13Y in preference combination A & combination B shows 2X & 9Y & so on as good X is increasing, the quantity of Good Y is decreasing. Joining al combinations from A to E, we get a curve which is downward sloping & convex to the origin known as Indifference curve or equal satisfaction curve. In this exchange the MRS is diminishing.

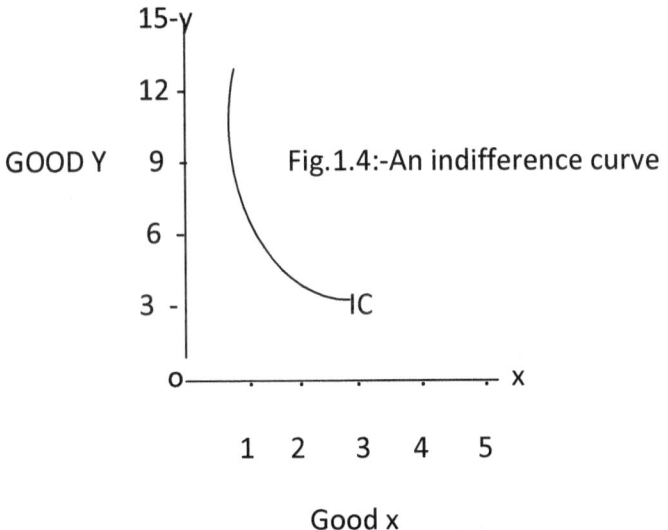

Fig.1.4:-An indifference curve

Good x

Properties/Features/Characteristics of Indifference Curves:-1.Downward sloping:-The ICs are downward sloping that is negative sloping indicating that as one good increase, other decreases. No other slope is possible as upward slope would mean both goods X& Y are increasing as in fig.1.5b & slope parallel to ox-axis mean good Y is kept constant & good x has no limit as in fig.1.5c & parallel to y-axis would mean opposite as in fig.1.5d, so the possible slope is negative as shown in fig. 1.5a.

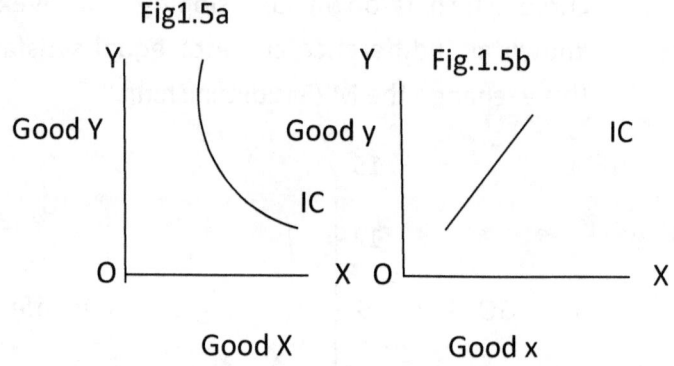

Fig1.5a

Fig.1.5b

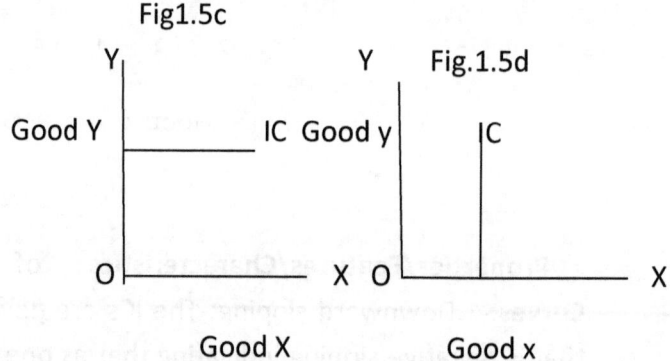

Fig1.5c

Fig.1.5d

2.Convex to the origin:-The ICs are convex to the origin , because MRS is diminishing, so no the shape is possible as convex shape would mean MRS is increasing & straight line

would mean MRS is constant as shown in figures 1.6a, b, &
c respectively.

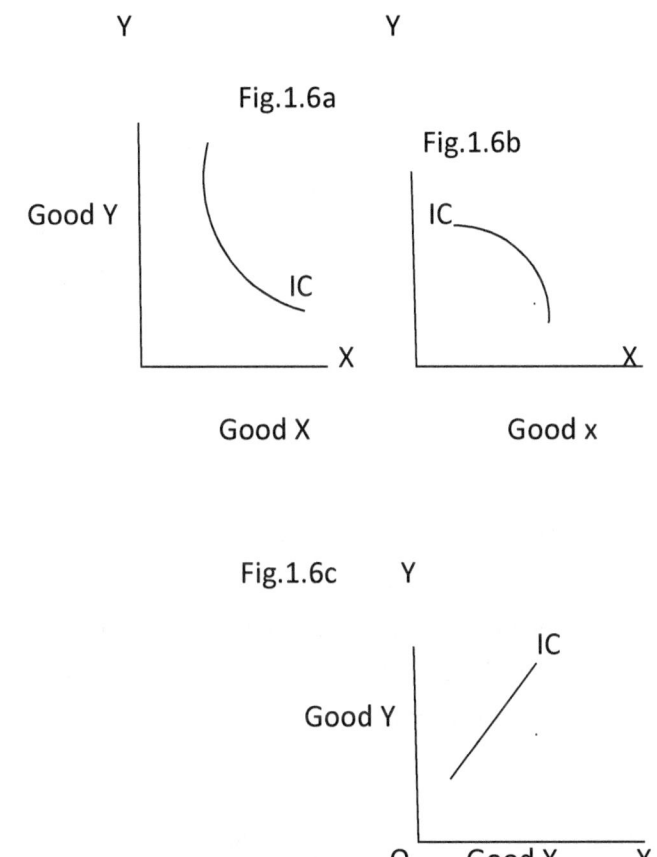

Fig.1.6a

Fig.1.6b

Fig.1.6c

3.Higher IC gives higher satisfaction:-This means more
combinations at higher level than at lower level IC so higher
the IC ,higher will be the satisfaction as shown in figure
below:-IC3 give more satisfaction than IC2 & IC1.

Fig.1.7:-Higher indifference curve ,higher satisfaction

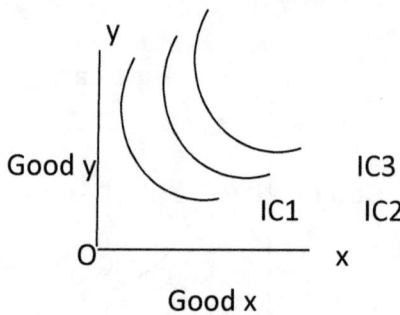

4. Two ICs cannot touch or intersect each other:-This because of transitivity meaning if preference A is better than preference B,B is better than C ,than for the same consumer A should be superior to C, so in the figure touch point is an absurd preference.

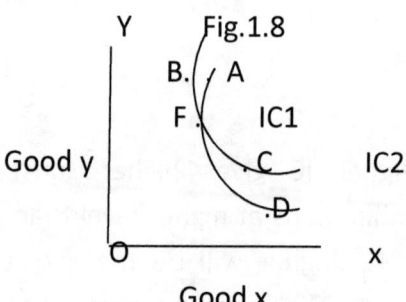

In figure 1.8 preference A can be better than B, C better than D, but F is non-sense.

5. ICs for perfect substitutes are parallel lines:-ICs for the perfect substitute good are parallel straight lines as shown in the figure1.9 below

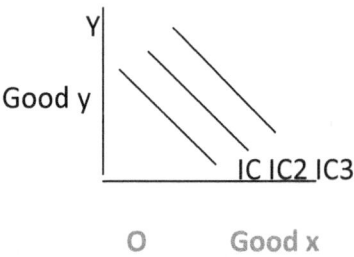

Figure 1.9: ICs for perfect substitute goods

5. ICs for perfect complements are right angles:-ICs are for perfectly complementary goods are right angles because they have joint demand as shown in figure1.10 below:

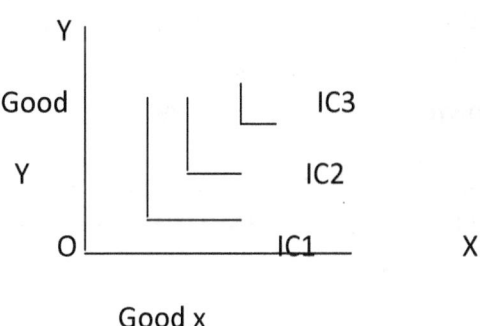

Figure 1.10 IC for complementary goods

6.ICs for bads are backward bending:-If good is not favorable or normal as some poisonous good, then IC curve for such good will be backward bending as shown in the figure1.11 below :

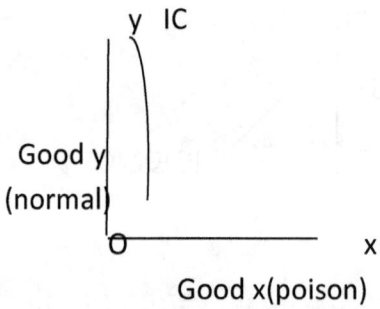

Figure 1.11:IC for bad good

MRS(Marginal Rate of Substitution):-MRS can be defined as the rate at which one good is exchanged for the other, for instance if the consumer has two goods say X & Y, then the rate at which two are exchanged for each other is called MRS. as shown in the equation below:

MRS=ΔY/ΔX, where ΔY is the loss of good Y to gain one unit of X as ΔX.Simply MRS is the price of one good in terms of another good.

Explanation: MRS can be explained with the help of table & diagram:

Table1.4(a):-MRS

Combination	Good X	Good Y	MRS
A	1	13	-
B	2	9	4
C	3	6	3
D	4	4	2
E	5	3	1

The table shows as good X increases with the consumer, good Y falls as combination A is 1X+13Y, as the consumer increases the good X by exchange, good Y falls as in combination B,2X+9Y,here 4 units of Y are lost, again in combination C,3units of Y are lost & so on. This shows diminishing MRS.

Diagrammatical presentation: Fig.1.11(a):-Diminishing MRS

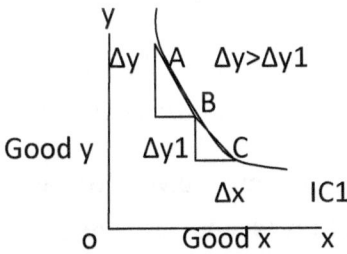

In figure1.11(a) Good X is taken along ox-axis& Good Y along oy-axis.IC1 is indifference curve on which the MRS is measured as movement from point A to B, where Good Y is lost to gain the Good X ,but the rate of loss is diminishing as the consumer moves to point C as Δy>Δy1.

Reasons for diminishing MRS:MRS is diminishing because:

1.The consumer does want the other good to be lost totally.

2.One good has full satisfying power.

3.Two goods can not act as substitutes for each other.

Consumer`s equilibrium through Hicks-Allen Approach:-

Consumer`s equilibrium is at a point where he gets maximum satisfaction from the purchases of any two goods given the prices & income.

Assumptions:- 1.Utility is an ordinal concept. That is rankable & not numerically measurable.

2. MRS is diminishing. It means as the exchange takes between the two goods the consumer does not want one good to go zero level.

3. Consumer is rational in nature. It means consumer can & do make choice & he/she always prefers more to less.

4. Prices, income   given for the consumer. It means during analysis they will not change & remain constant.

5. Ordering is weak. It indicates the consumer can prefer choice A to choice B & vice-versa.

6. Preference is indifference. It means the consumer can prefer choice A to choice B or reverse or prefer both equally.

7. Preference is complete. It means consumer can make complete preference order.

8. Consistency:-It means if in one situation A is preferred to B, in next situation reverse is not possible.

9. Transitivity:-It implies if consumer says A is better than B & B than C, that means A is better than C, so it should not possible that C is better than B or A.

Explanation:-The consumer equilibrium can be explained with the help of following tools:

a. Indifference map:-The set of various indifference curves is known as indifference map as shown in the figure1.12 below:-

Fig.1.12:-Indifference Map

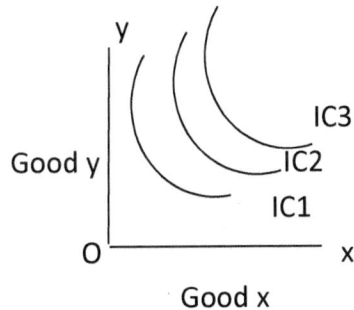

b. Budget line:-The price −income line or budget constraint line by which the consumer can make purchases for any combination of two goods. Let the income of the consumer be equal to Rs100, price of good X per unit is Rs10 & that of good Y is Rs10 per unit, so either 10x or 10y goods can be purchased if the Rs100 is spent on the good X or good Y.Thus line joining 10x & 10y is the budget line in the graph given below.

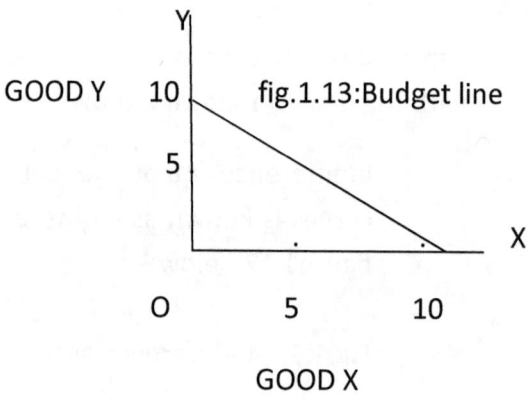

fig.1.13:Budget line

GOOD X

Equilibrium point:-For the equilibrium point we bring the indifference map & the budget line together as shown in the figure below:-In the figure 1.14:-

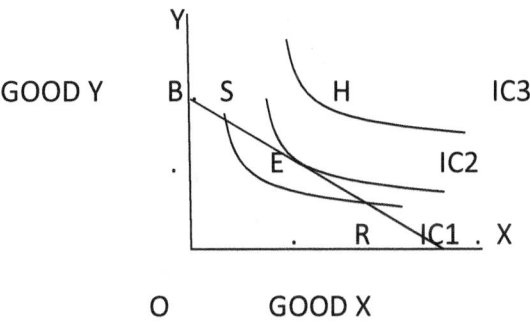

Fig.1.14 Consumer`s equilibrium

1.Along OX-axis we have taken good x & along OY-axis we have taken good y.

2.BL is the budget line of the consumer & IC1,2,3 are the indifference curves for the consumer.

3.E is the equilibrium point where the budget line is tangent to the IC2,because

 a. The budget line is tangent to the IC2.

b.The IC2 is convex to the origin.

c.The slope of the IC2 & the budget line are equal i.e. slope of BL at point E =Perpendicular/Base, so it is M/Py/M/Px as under

=M/Py/M/Px=Px/Py, where M is money income, P is price& Y are goods.

4. As these conditions are not satisfied at point s & R, hence equilibrium not possible & point H is not reachable for lack of budget.

Elasticity of Demand(Ed):-As the demand is mainly affected by the price of the good in question, price of the(p), related goods(Pr),income of the consume(Y)r, so elasticity measures the effect, thus Ed is the response of the demand in response to the percentage change in the P,Pr &Y,calculated as

Ed=   %age change in quantity demanded/%age change in P,Pr,y

Thus Ed is of three types:-

a. **Price elasticity (ep):-**ep can be defined as the percentage change in the quantity demanded divided by the percentage change in price, as

ep(-)=   %age change in quantity demanded /%age change   in   Price   of   the   good

Δ

ep(-)=$\Delta q/q \times 100$ / $\Delta p/p \times 100$

=$\Delta q/\Delta p \times p/q$.

Where   eP is price elasticity of demand, Δ p is change in price as p-p1 & Δ q is change in quantity as q-q1 ,p is original price ,q is original quantity. Give any four values ,5th can be found out,-ve sign means price & demand has inverse relation & ignored for simplicity.

Degrees/types of ep:-eP is of following five types/degrees:-

1.Perfectly elastic demand(eP=∞):-ep is said to be perfectly elastic when at the give price demand is infinite & the demand curve is parallel to the ox-axis as shown in the figure1.15:-

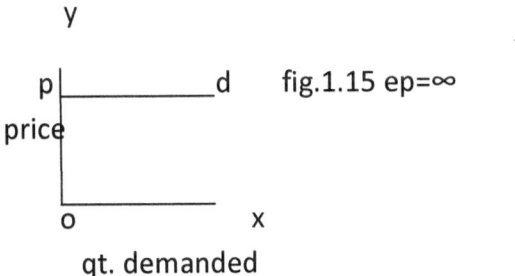

fig.1.15 ep=∞

2 Perfectly elastic demand(Ep=0):-Ep is said be perfectly inelastic when whatever the change in price causes no change in the quantity demanded, here the demand curve is parallel to the oy-axis as shown in the figure1.16 :

Whether price falls to p1 or rises to p2 from op, quantity remains the same i.e.oq.

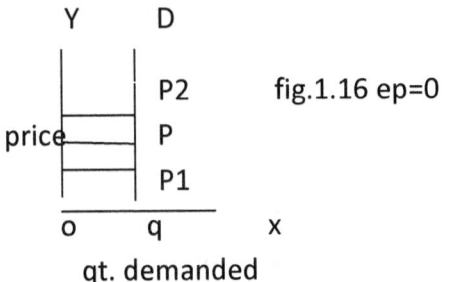

fig.1.16 ep=0

3.Relatively or more than unitary elastic(ep>1):-ep is said to be more than unitary when percentage change in price causes more percentage change in quantity demanded, as shown in the figure1.17 below:-herepp1 is less than qq1.

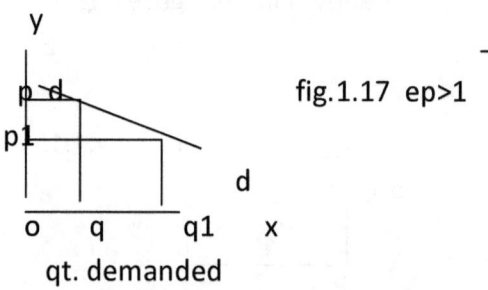

fig.1.17 ep>1

4.Relatively or less than unitary elastic(ep<1):-ep is said to be more than unitary when percentage change in price causes less percentage change in quantity demanded, as shown in the figure 1.18 below:-here pp1 is more than qq1.

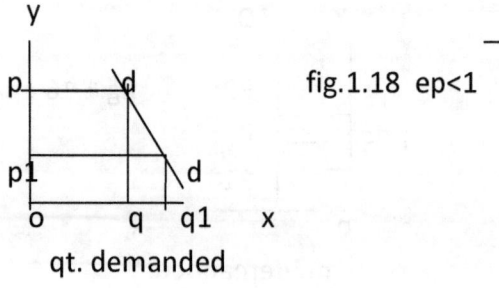

fig.1.18 ep<1

5. unitary elastic(ep=1):-ep is said to be unitary when percentage changein price causes equal percentage change in quantity demanded,as shown in the figure 1.19 below:-here pp1 is equal to qq1.

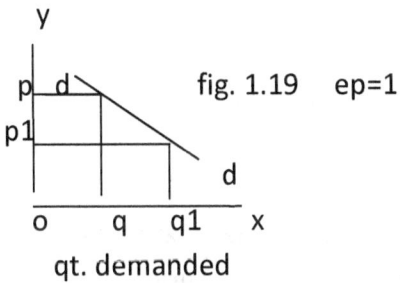

fig. 1.19   ep=1

qt. demanded

Measuring ep:- There are five methods to measure the ep as under:-

1.**Percentage /Mathematical method**:-According to this method ep can be defined as the percentage change in the quantity demanded divided by the percentage change in price, as

eP(-)=   %age change in quantity demanded/%age change in Price of the good

eP(-)=Δq/q ×100 / Δp/p ×100

$$=\Delta q/\Delta p \times p/q.$$

Where eP is price elasticity of demand, Δ p is change in price as p-p1 & Δ q is change in quantity as q-q1 ,p is original price ,q is original quantity.Give any four values ,5th can be found out,-ve sign means price & demand has inverse relation & ignored for simplicity.

For instance if price of ice cream falls from Rs15 to Rs10 & quantity rises from 5 to 10 units ,then ep will be

$$Ep=\frac{\Delta q \times p}{\Delta p \times q}=\frac{5 \times 15}{5 \times 5}=3 \text{ i.e. more than unitary.}$$

2.**Total outlay/expenditure method**:-When we multiply the price & quantity,we get the expenditure,so for measuring ep ,initial & final expenditure is compared.This method measures the ep under following three cases:-

1.ep>1:-when final expenditure or outlay is more than initial in case of fall in price of the good in question,ep is more than unitary as.

  Price × quantity =Expenditure

Rs 10 × 8   =Rs80 ⎤ Initial   As final expenditure is more, so ep is >1⎦

Rs8 × 12   =Rs96 Final

2.ep<1:-when final expenditure or outlay is less than initial in case of fall in price of the good in question,ep is less than unitary as.

Price × quantity =Expenditure

Rs 10 ×   8   =Rs80 ⎤ Initial   As final
expenditure is less, so ep is <1. ⎦
Rs8 ×   9   =Rs72 Final

3.ep=1:-when final expenditure or outlay is equal to initial in case of fall or rise in price of the good in question,ep is less than unitary as.

Price × quantity =Expenditure

Rs 9 × 8   =Rs72 Initial ⎤
Rs8 ×   9   =Rs72 Final ⎦
As final expenditure is equal to the initial, so ep is =1.

Diagrammaticall,the expenditure method can be reflected as:

In figure 1.20 along ox-axis we have taken price & along oy-axis expenditure & the three cases are as

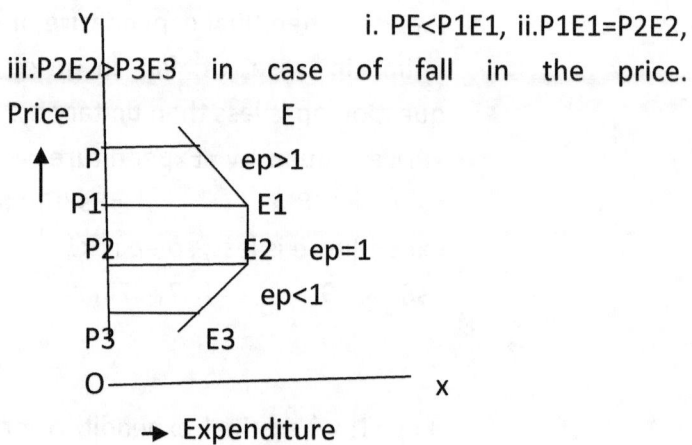

i. PE<P1E1, ii.P1E1=P2E2, iii.P2E2>P3E3 in case of fall in the price.

Fig.1.20:Total outlay Method

3.Point/Geometrical Method:-In this method point elasticity is calculated at any point of the demand curve, hence demand curve is used as in the figure 1.21:-

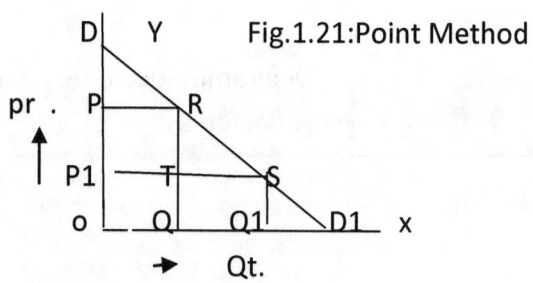

Fig.1.21:Point Method

According to percentage method

$$ep = \Delta q \times p / \Delta p \times q = \text{----}(1)$$ because
$$RT = PP1(\Delta p), ST = QQ1(\Delta q)$$

As Δs RTS & PDR are similar ,therefore ST/RT=RP/PD
& RP=OQ

$$\therefore ep = \frac{ST}{RT} \times \frac{OP}{OQ}$$

$$\therefore ep = \frac{OQ}{PD} \times \frac{OP}{OQ} ===>$$

∴ ep =OP/PD   BECAUSE OP=RQ, so   ep=RQ/PD

Again Δs PDR & RPD1 are similar, so $\frac{RQ}{PD} = \frac{RD1}{RD}$

∴.ep=RD1/RD   i.e. Lower segment of DDcurve/Upper segment

Calculating   point   elasticity   on   Demand
Curve:-Using above formula,ep can be calculated as

1.ep at point D=$\frac{DD1}{0} = \frac{4}{0} = \infty$

$$2.\text{ep at point B} = \frac{BD1}{BD} = \frac{3}{1} = \text{ep} > 1$$

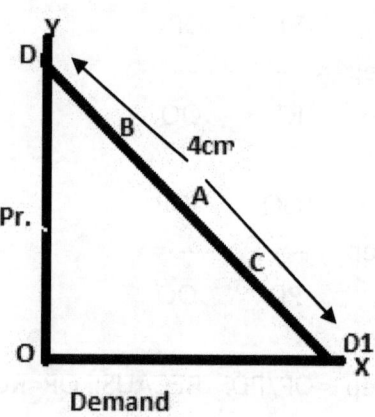

Figure 1.22 :Measuring ep with point method

$$3.\text{ep at point A} = \frac{AD1}{AD} = \frac{2}{2} = 1$$

$$4.\text{ep at point C} = \frac{CD1}{CD} = \frac{1}{3} = 0.33 \text{ ,i.e. less than 1}$$

$$5.\text{ep at D1} = \frac{0}{DD1} = \frac{0}{4} = 0$$

4.Arc elasticity method:-This method was given by Sir Dalton. According to this method ,average of price & quantity is taken instead of original price & quantity.This method has merit because at arc , point method can not be used as arc is greater than than straight line between any two points of DD curve,thus

According to percent method,

$ep= \Delta q /\Delta p \times p/q$

So, in arc method we replace,p/q by average of p+p1/ average ofq+q1,i.e.

$$Ep = \frac{\Delta q}{\Delta p} \times \dots \dots \frac{p+p1/2}{q+q1/2}$$

$$ep = \frac{\Delta q}{\Delta p} \times \dots \dots \frac{p+p1}{q+q1}$$

Where p is original price,p1 is new price & q is original quantity ,q1 is new quantity.

In figure 1.23 arc AB is more than AB straight line average
is used.

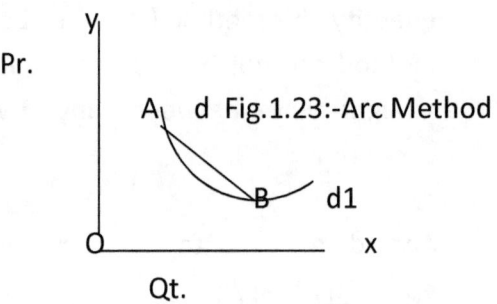

Fig.1.23:-Arc Method

5.**Average Revenue(AR) Method**:-This method was given by Lady Robinson worked on imperfect market and found the ep & AR relation as

ep=AR/AR-MR, thus explained with the help diagram as under:-

In figure 1.24 along ox-axis is quantity & along oy-axis is price,AR &MR are average & marginal revenue which are downward sloping for imperfect market.

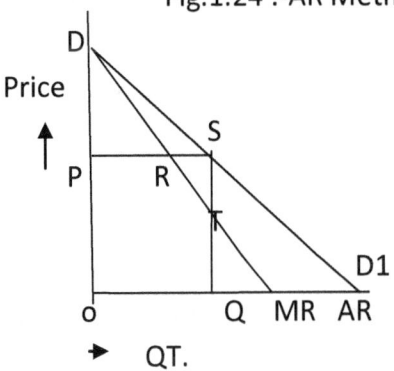
Fig.1.24 :-AR Method

According to point method ,ep at point S=SD1/SD, as ∆sSPD &SQD1 are similar so we can writeSD1/SD=SQ /PD.

Again ∆PDS & SRT are similar by AAA Rule, so we can say ST=PD,Thus

Ep=SQ/PD =SQ/ST=SQ/SQ-TQ=AR/AR-MR

So,Ep= AR/AR-MR where AR is average revenue & MR is marginal revenue.

b.**cross elasticity(ec)**:-Cross elasticity can be defined as the percentage change in quantity demanded of a good say X in response to the percentage change in price of the other good say Y.i.e.

$$Ce= \Delta qx/qx/ \Delta py/py$$

where∆ qx means change in quantity of x,qx is original quantity,∆py is change in price of good y, py is original price of y.

Types:-It can be of following types

a.positive ec:-if both demand and price move in the same direction as in case of substitute goods as coagate toothpaste & pepsodent paste.

b.negative ec:-if the demand & price move in opposite direction as in case of the complements pen & ink.

c.zero cross elasticity:-if the price of one good has no effect on the other as in unrelated goods.e.g. pen & shoes.

c.**Income elasticity (ey)**:-It can be defined as the percentage change in qt. demanded of a good with respect to the percentage change in income of the consumer .ey can be expressed as

$$ey = \frac{\Delta q/q \times 100}{\Delta y/y \times 100} = \frac{\Delta q \times y}{\Delta y \times q}$$

Where Δq is change in quantity & Δy is change in income ,y is original income,q is original quantity.

Types:-It can be

a. Positive ey:-If the demand & income move in the same direction, making positive sloped demand curve as shown below.

Fig.1.25:Positive ey

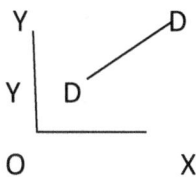

b.Negative ey:- If the demand & income move in the opposite direction, making negative sloped demand curve as shown below. Fig1.26: Negative ey

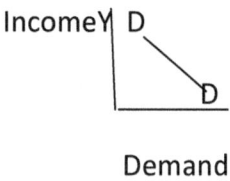

Demand

Fig.1.26:Negative eY

c.   Zero ey:- ey is zero if the demand does not change due to change in income, making vertical sloped demand curve as show n below.Fig1.27 ,zero ey

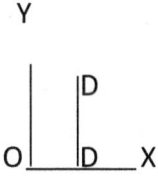

Fig.1.27 ,Zero ey

Factors affecting Ed:-

The Ed depends on following factors:-

1.Nature of the good:-If the good is necessary e.g. rice,dal, demand is inelastic, but if the goods are luxuries as AC,refrigerators etc demand will be elastic. For comforts as milk ,fruits etc demand is moderate.

2.Price of the good: If the price is very high as diamond & very low as match box, demand is inelastic & for middle price ranged goods demand is elastic.

3.Income of the consumer:- For the very rich & very poor people the demand inelastic because for rich prices matter not & for the poor, they demand their needs which are less. But for middle class the demand ids elastic.

4.Shifting of the consumption:-If the consumption can be shifted for the future after price rise e.g. juice, demand is elastic but where consumption can not be shifted e.g. cooking gas, kerosene oil etc demand is inelastic.

5.Habbit of the consumer:-If the consumer is habitual or addict as smokers & drinkers, demand is inelastic but where addiction is not the case demand is elastic.

6.Time period:-Longer the time with the consumer, he can adjust demand, so elastic but in the short period he cannot shift the demand e.g. cooking gas, so demand is inelastic.

Consumer Surplus(CS):-Thev concept of CS was given by a French engineer,Dupuit in 1944 & introduced in economics in 1890 by Sir Marshall.

Meaning;-According to the concept CS, willingness to pay for goods & services is more than the market price, hence this more is the CS.Thus CS is the willingness to pay minus the market price,i.e.

CS=WILLINGNESS TO PAY-ACTUAL MARKET PRICE, for instance if consumer goes to market to purchase a pair of shoes for him,thinking that it would be for Rs2500, but actually he found it at Rs2000, so CS will be as

CS=Rs2500-Rs2000=Rs500

Assumptions:-same as for cardinal utility.

Explanation:-The CS can be explained with table & diagram as under:

Table 1.5:-CS

Units of good	MU(willingness)	Actual price	CS
1	50	10	40
2	40	10	30
3	30	10	20
4	20	10	10
5	10	10	0
Total	150	50	100

In the table 1.5, unit wise willingness(MU) & actual price has been shown to find tha CS, for the 1st unit it isRs 40, for 2nd it is Rs30 & so on goes to zero for 5th unit.Total willingness to pay for all units is Rs150,total actual price for all units is Rs50, so CS is Rs100.

Diagrammtically,CS can be represented as under:-In figure along ox-axis is the demand & along oy-axis is the price,DD is the demand curve,FOR OQ qt. the consumer is ready to pay OD, but he gets it at price OP,so PD is surplus as calculated under:-

CS=arODEQ-arOQEP=arPDE.

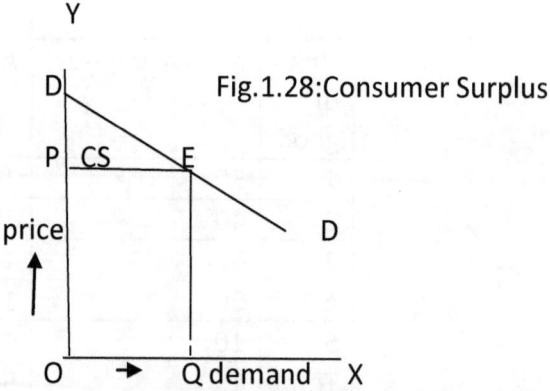

Fig.1.28:Consumer Surplus

Usefulness/utility/importance:-

1.It solved water-diamond paradox,i.e. why diamond is heavily priced without which life is possibe & water is free without which life is not possible as MU is high for diamond.

2.Guides the finance minister in tax –expenditure policy as rich have low Mum as compared to the poor.

3.Guides the government policy to provide socio-economic facilities to the consumers,as much CS is enjoyed in these provisions.

Criticism:-1.Based on cardinal utility analysis, which is not valid.

2.It is an imaginary concept because willingnee to pay need not to be more than the price.

3.It is difficult to measure in many cases.

4.In many cases it can be zero or even negative.

*********** ....

Unit-2nd

Production function:-

Tits-bits:

Production: To produce the goods & services with the help of factors of production.

Factors of Production: They are land, labour, capital & the entrepreneur.

Stock &Supply: Stock is the total quantity available with the seller at a point of time & the supply is the part of stock offered for sale.

Production function (PF): It is the functional relationship between the physical inputs & the output.

Law of variable proportion: The short run production function when only one or two factor inputs are variable & others kept constant to get the output. The output is variable as first increases, then becomes maximum & finally declines.

Returns to scale: The long run production function when output is the result of change in all factor inputs.

Time factor: It can be short run say 1-5years, medium run 5-10years & the long run 10plus years.

Economies & diseconomies of Scale: They refer to the benefits (economies) & losses (diseconomies).

Isoquant: The curve which shows equal satisfaction for the producer on all its points.

TC, AC, MC: TC is the total cost,i.e, the expenditure in producing the total output.AC is the average cost calculated as AC=TC/n, where n is the number of units of the factor input.MC is the cost due to the additional unit output & calculated as MC=ΔTC/Δn, where Δ is change.

Producer`s Equlibrium: The point when the producer has the maximum profits & minimum costs.

Expansion path: The line joining the various equilibrium points showing maximum output & least cost.

Economic region: The region which shows marginal productivity of the factors positive or zero.

Ridge lines: The lines which bound the economic region & where on these lines the marginal factor productivity is zero.

Iso-cost line: The line which shows equal cost on all its points.

Total cost: It is the total cost incurred in the production process including both the fixed & the variable cost.

Money cost:It is the cost in monetary terms.

Opportunity cost: It is the cost of opportunity lost.

Fixed cost: It is the cost on fixed factors of production in the short run.

Variable cost: It is the cost on the variable factors of production in the short run.

Production Indifference Curve/Isoquant & Properties/Features/Characteristics of Producer Indifference Curves

Producer Indifference Curve/Isoquant /Equal product curve:-The curve which shows producer's prefence schedule for the different combinations of any two factors.This curve gives equal satisfaction to the producer on all its points indication different combinations of any two factors of production.

Explanation:-The isoquant can be explained with the help of a table & diagram as under:-

Table2.1:-Indifference Curve

Combination	Labour(L)	Capital(K)	MRTS
A	1	13	-
B	2	9	4
C	3	6	3
D	4	4	2
E	5	3	1

The table 2.1 shows 1L & 13K in preference combination A & combination B shows 2L & 9K & so on as labour is increasing, the quantity of capital is decreasing. In this exchange the MRTS is decreasing from 4 to 1.

Diagramattical Presentation:- The figure 2.1 shows 1L & 13K in preference combination A & combination B shows 2L & 9K & so on as L is increasing, the quantity of K is decreasing. Joining al combinations from A to E, we get a curve which is downward sloping & convex to the origin known as Producer Indifference curve or equal satisfaction curve or isoquant. In this exchange the MRTS is diminishing.

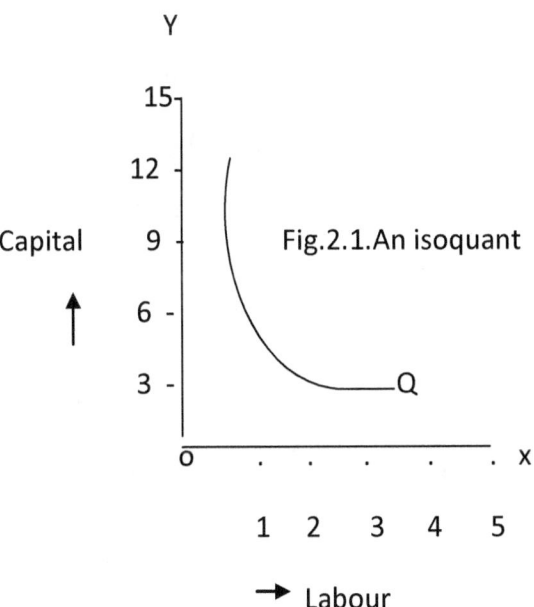

Fig.2.1.An isoquant

Properties/Features/Characteristics of Indifference Curves:-

1.Downward sloping:-The IQs are downward sloping that is negative sloping indicating that as one factor increases, other decreases. No other slope is possible as upward slope would mean both L & K are increasing as in fig.2.2 b & slope parallel to ox-axis mean capital is kept constant & labour has no limit as in fig.2.2 c & parallel to y-axis would mean opposite as in fig. 2.2d, so the possible slope is negative as shown in fig. 2.2a.

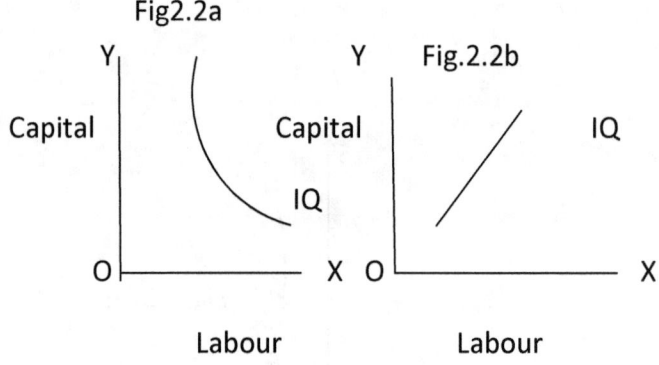

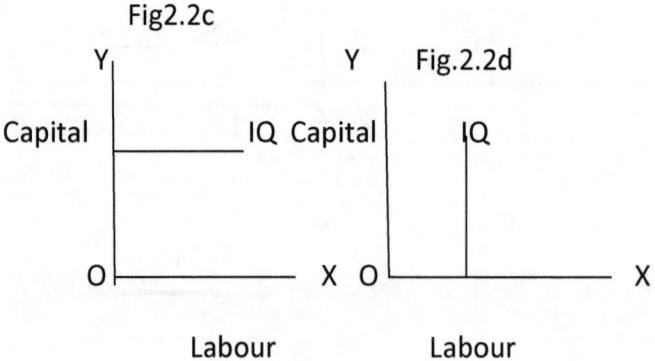

2.Convex to the origin:-The IQs are convex to the origin , because MRTS is diminishing, so no the shape is possible as convex shape would mean MRTS is increasing & straight line would mean MRTS is constant as shown in figures 2.3a, 2.3b, & 2.3c respectively.

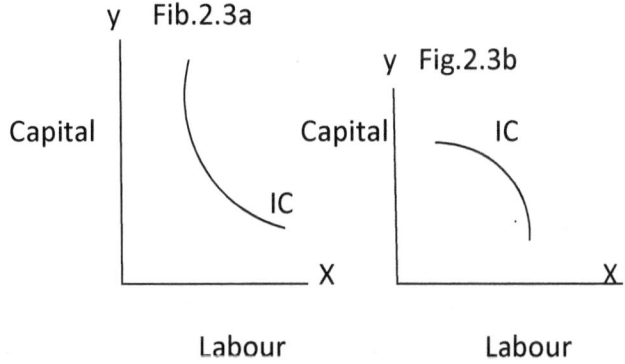

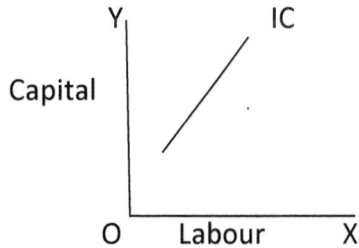

Fig.2.3c

3.Higher IQ gives higher satisfaction:-This means more production at higher level than at lower level IC so higher the

IQ ,higher will be the satisfaction as shown in figure below:-
IQ3 give more

Satisfaction than IC2 & IC1.   Fig.2.4

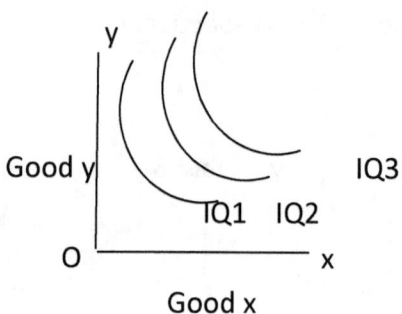

Good x

4.Two IQs cannot touch or intersect each other:-This because of transitivity meaning if preference A is better than preference B,B is better than C ,than for the same producer A should be superior to C, so in the figure touch point is an absurd preference.

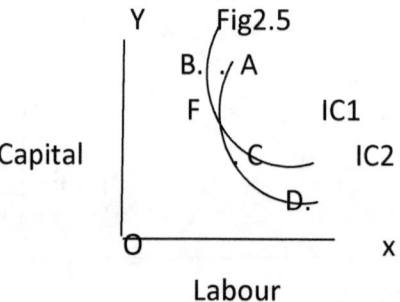

Labour

In figure 2.5, preference A can be better than B ,C better than D, but F is non-sense.

5. IQs for perfect substitutes are parallel lines:-IQs for the perfect substitute factors are parallel straight lines as shown in the figure below

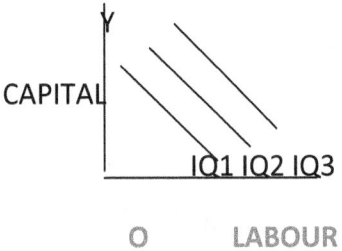

Figure 2.6 for perfect substitute goods

6. IQs for perfect complements are right angled:-IQs are for perfectly complementary factors are right angles because they have joint demand as shown in figure below:

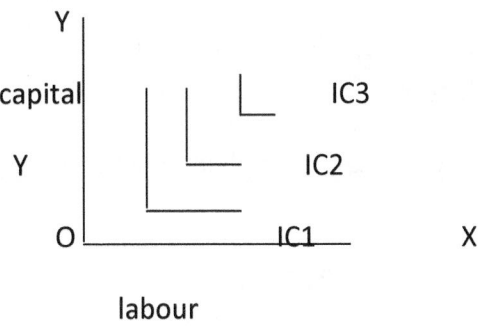

Figure 2.7:IQ for complementary goods

7.IQs for bads are backward bending:-If factor is not favorable or inefficient, then IQ curve for such factor will be backward bending as shown in the figure below :

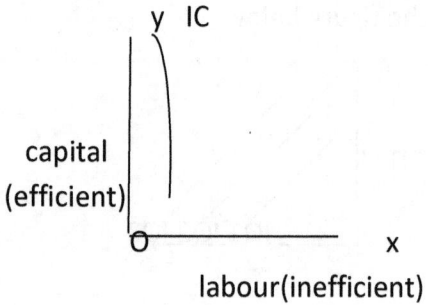

Figure 2.8:IQ for bad Factors

MRTS(Marginal Rate Technical of Substitution):-MRTS can be defined as the rate at which one factor is exchanged for the other, for instance if the producerer has two factors say labour(L) & capital(K), then the rate at which two are exchanged for each other is called MRTS. as shown in the equation below:

MRTS=$\Delta K/\Delta L$, where ΔK is the loss of factor ,K to gain one unit of L as ΔL.Simply MRTS is the price of one factor in terms of another factor.

Explanation: MRTS can be explained with the help of table & diagram:

Table2.1(a):-MRTS

Combination	Labour (L)	Capital K	MRTS
A	1	13	-
B	2	9	4

C	3	6	3
D	4	4	2
E	5	3	1

The table 2.1(a) shows as L increases with the producer, K falls as combination A is 1L+13K, as the producer increases the L by exchange, K falls as in combination B,2L+9K,here 4 units of K are lost, again in combination C,3units of K are are lost & so on.This shows diminishing MRTS.

Diagrammatical presentation:

Fig.2.8(a):-Diminishing MRTS

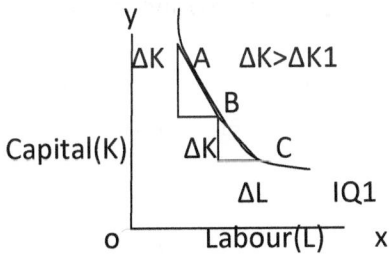

In figure 2.8(a) Labour,L is taken along ox-axis& Capital,K along oy-axis.IQ1 is Isoquant curve on which the MRTS is measured as movement from point A to B, where K is lost to gain the L ,but the rate of loss is diminishing as the producer moves to point C as Δk>ΔK1.

Reasons for diminishing MRTS: MRTS is diminishing because:

1. The producer does not want the other factor to be lost totally.

2. One factor has a limit,so other factor is also required.

3. Two factors cannot act as substitutes for each other.

Producer`s equilibrium:- Hicks-Allen Approach/Ordinal approach:-

Producer`s equilibrium is at a point where he gets maximum satisfaction from the production using any two factors of production the factor prices & income of the producer.

Assumptions:-

Explanation:-The producer equilibrium can be explained with the help of following tools:

a.**Isoquant map:-**The set of various isoquants is known as isoquant map as shown in the figure 2.9 below:-

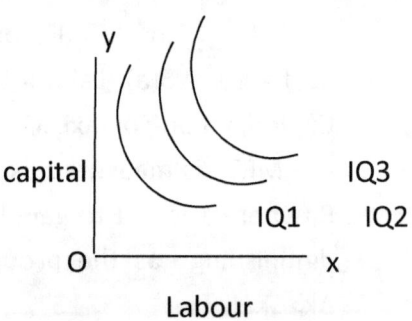

Fig.2.9:Isoquant Map

b.**Budget line/Iso-cost line:-**The factor price –income line or budget constraint/iso-cost line by which the producer can employ any combination of two factors,known as iso-cost line because cost equally for anyl combination . Let the income of the producer be equal to Rs100, price of labour per unit is Rs10 & that of capital is Rs10 per unit, so either 10L or 10K can be employed if the Rs100 is spent on the labour or capital.Thus line joining 10L & 10k is the budget line/iso-cost line in the graph given below.

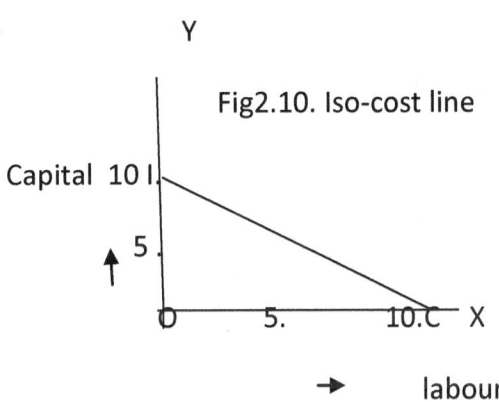

Fig2.10. Iso-cost line

Equilibrium point:-For the equilibrium point we bring the isoquant map & the iso-cost line together as shown in the figure below:-In the figure2.11:-

1.Along OX-axis we have taken labour & along OY-axis we have taken capital.

2.IC is the Iso-cost line of the producer & IQ1,2,3 are the producer indifference curves .

3.E is the equilibrium point where the Iso-cost line is tangent to the IQ2,because

a. The iso-cost line is tangent to the IQ2.

b.the IQ2 is convex to the origin.

c.the slope of the IQ2 & the ISO-COST line are equal i.e. slope of IC at point E =PERPENDICULAR/BASE, so it is M/p(k)/M/P(l) as under

=M/P(k)/M/P(l)=P(l)/P(k),where M is money income ,P(l) is price of labour& p(k) price of capital.

4.As these conditions are not satisfied at point s & R, hence equilibrium not possible & point H is not reachable for lack of budget.

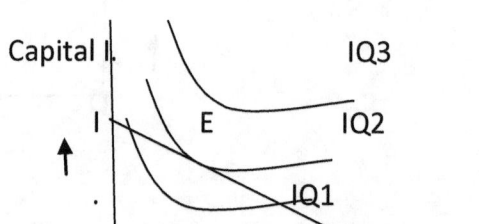

y   Fig.2.11: Least cost combination

Fig.2.11: Least cost combination/producer`s equilibrium

Expansion Path:-The firm or the producer is in the equilium ,whe it attains the least cost combination, i.e. the point where the isoquant .The line joining such various equilibrium points with expanding production   is known as the expansion path as shown in the figure below:

In figure 2.12:

1.along ox-axix we have taken labou,along oy-axis capital units.

2.IC1,IC2,IC3 are the iso-cost lines & IQ1,IQ2,IQ3 are the isoquants.

3.E1, E2, E3 are the equilibrium points showing least cot combination for the firm.

 The line joining all the equilibrium points is known as the expansion path.

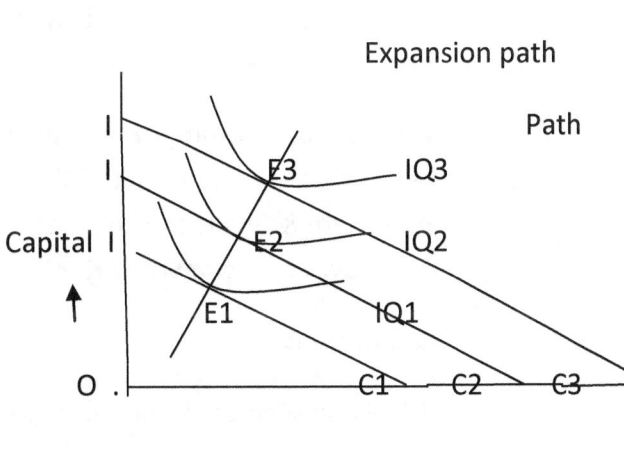

Y

Expansion path

Path

E3 ── IQ3

Capital E2 ── IQ2

E1 IQ1

O C1 C2 C3

→ labour

Production Function:-The functional relationship between the inputs & the output is known as the production function.AS there are five factor inputs as land ,labour, capital, entrepreneur,technology .Their employment in the production process gives output.This is what called as the production function(PF)

Depending upon time period it is of two types:

1.Short Run Production function(SRPF)   **2.Long run production function(LRPF)**

 1.Short Run Production function(SRPF):-Usually 1-5 year period is short in production process, hence in the short run only one or two factors can be changed not all.So the output is the result of one factor say labour, others remain unchanged or fixed.Thus it is known as the law of returns to a factor, as the returns are variable & diminishing , so the SRPF is also known as the Law of Diminishing Returns or the Law ofVariable Proportions(quantities).

Law of Diminishing Returns:-According to this law the returns to a factor initially increase, then they become maximum & finally they decline.Thus the returns are variable ,so known as the **lawof variable proportions.**

Assumtions:-

1.Only one factor say labour is variable, other factors remain constant.

2.The technology will remain the same

3.The law is valid in the short run.

Explanation:-The law can be explained with the help of table & diagram as under:

Table 2.2:Law of diminishing returns

Units of Labour	Total Product(TP)	Average Product(AP)	Marginal Product(MP)	Returns stage
1	4	4	4	1st stage >ing returns
2	9	4.5	5	
3	15	5	6	
4	20	5	5	2nd stage constant returns
5	20	4	0	
6	18	3	-2	3rd stage negative returns

In the table, when 1st unit of labur is employed,TP is 4units,AP is 4,MP is also 4 units, when 3rd unit of labour is employed, TP rises to 15units, so AP &MP to 5units & 6units respectively.However at 4th unit of labour TP slows & becomes maximum at 5th unit.

Following TP,AP& MP are also slowing but MP becomes zero.Further at 6th unit of labour TP stars declining, thus AP

& MP also but MP becomes negative.Thus there are three stage, i.e. increasing returns in 1st, constant returns in 2nd & negative returns in 3rd.

Thus the production trend is variable,this explains the law.

Diagrammatical presentation:-

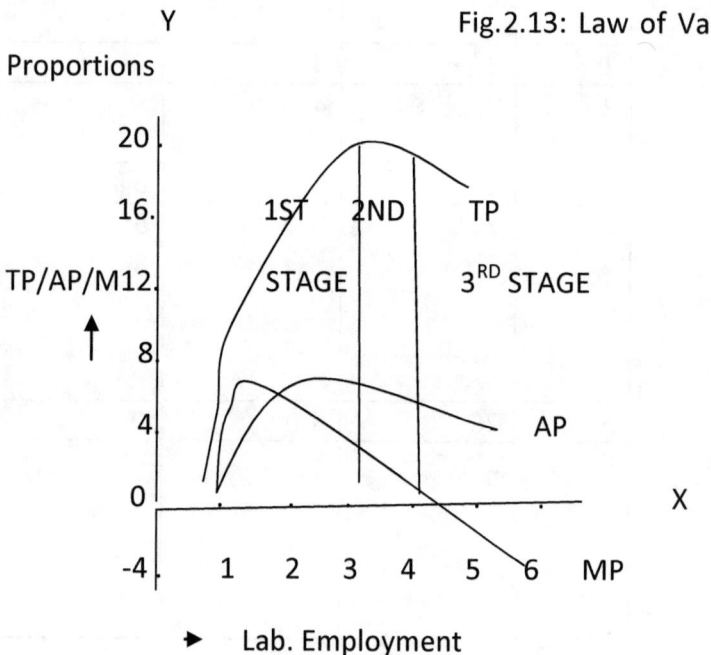

Fig.2.13: Law of Variable Proportions

In fig. 2.13:-

1.along ox-axis we have taken units of labour& along oy-axis TP,AP& MP.

2.TP,AP & MP are the total revenue, av. revenue,marginal reve. respectively.

3.the law operates under three stages,

a.1st stage,the increasing returns:-In this stage TP increases , following this AP, MP are also rising but MP is rising faster.

b.2nd stage,constant returns:-In this stage,TP reaches to maximum, following this AP, MP start falling, MP falls faster & becomes zero at the end of 2nd stage.However both AP & MP are positive.

c.3rd stage,negative returns:-In this stage TP starts declining, following this both AP& MP fall but MP falls faster & becomes negative.

Causes of the Law;-The law operates because,

1.More fixed factor: In the 1st stage the fixed factor is large, so adding more variable factor say labour increases the returns as in agriculture .

2.Efficiecy & experience:-As the more variable factor is employed, the repetitive activity increases efficiency & expertise of the workers ,so increasing returns.

3.Division of labour:-Bit by bit work fasters the speed of working & thus adding labour productivity.

4.Balanced combination:- In 2nd stage as the variable factor is further increased , a balance is reached where factor ratio becomes optimum & returns can`t increase further. This gives constant returns.

5.More variable factor:-In 3rd stage further addition of the variable factor brings negative returns as fixed factor becomes scarce, so added labour contributes nothing as in kitchen too many cooks spoil it.

6.Ineffeciency breeds in:-Excess variable factor with no or little work share brings inefficiency & thus negative returns.

Application of the law:-The law is applicable to all sectors of the economy be it agriculture, industry or service sector.

Criticism:-Technology can reverse the diminishing returns in the economy as experienced by the developed countries ,the USA, the UK etc.But the law assumes technology to remain unchanged.

Conclusion:-Despite conclusion , the law operate as the general trend in the third world countries, even in some developed world countries.

2.**Long run production function(LRPF)**:-In the long run usually more than 5 to 10 year period all factors of production can be changed ,i.e. entire scale is changeable ,so the returns are due to scale not one factor & called Returns to Scale(RTS).

Returns to Scale (RTS):-Returns to scale mean the response of the output to all the factor inputs which are variable in the long run. Here the contribution of all the factor inputs is taken into consideration. The RTS can be increasing, constant & decreasing depending upon the response of the returns.

Types of RTS:-

1. Increasing RTS:-The RTS are said to be increasing if the given percentage change in factor inputs causes more percentage change in the output.For instance if Rs50lac. Investment brings Rs80lac, then RTS are increasing.

    Graphical presentation:- Increasing RTS can be explained graphically as under,

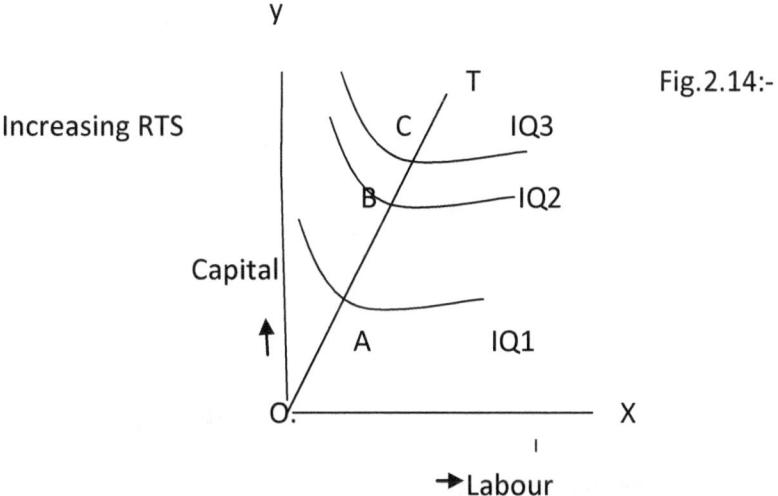

Fig.2.14:-

In figure 2.14:

1.along ox-axis we have taken labur & along oy-axis we have taken capital.

2.OT is the scale line, IQ1.IQ2,IQ3 are isoquant at decreasing distance,i.e OA>AB>BC.

3.decreasing distance means more output with less & less factor inputs.

2. Decreasing RTS:-The RTS are said to be decreasing if the given percentage change in factor input causes less percentage change in the output. For instance if Rs50lac Investment brings Rs30lac, then RTS are decreasing.

Graphical presentation:- decreasing RTS can be explained graphically as under,

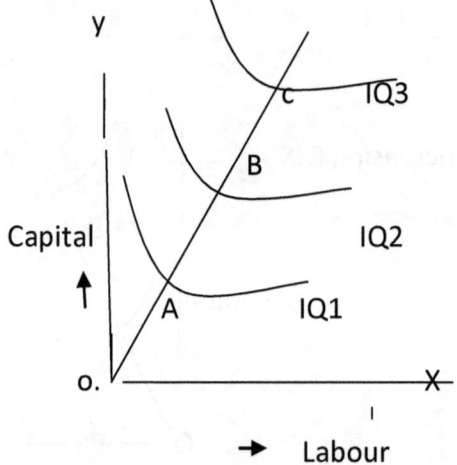

In figure 2.15 :

1.along ox-axis we have taken labor & along oy-axis we have taken capital.

2.OT is the scale line, IQ1.IQ2,IQ3 are isoquants at increasing distance,i.e OA<AB<BC.

3.Increasing distance means less output with more & more factor inputs.

3.Constant RTS:-The RTS are said to be constant if the given percentage change in factor inputs causes same percentage change in the output. For instance if Rs50lac. Investment brings Rs50lac, then RTS are constant.

Graphical presentation:- Constant RTS can be explained graphically as under,

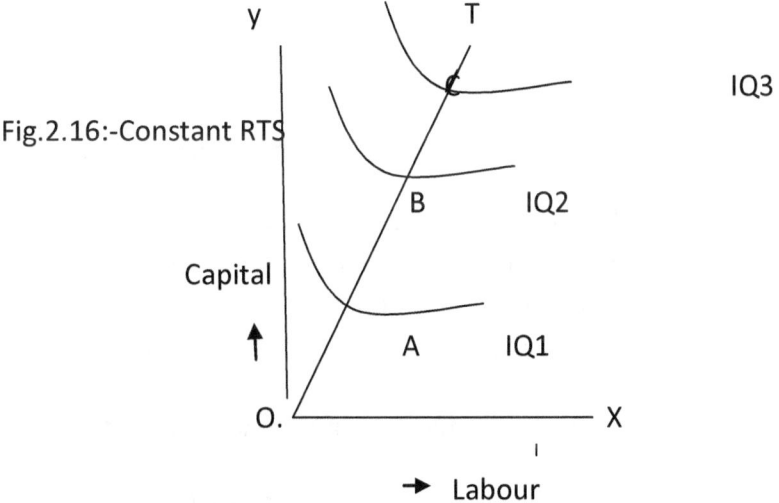

Fig.2.16:-Constant RTS

In figure 2.16:

1.along ox-axis we have taken labur & along oy-axis we have taken capital.

2.OT is the scale line, IQ1.IQ2,IQ3 are isoquants at equal distance,i.e OA=AB=BC.

3.Equal distance means same output with same factor inputs.

Causes of different types of RTS:- RTS are caused due to (A) economies &(B) diseconomies of scale.

1. When economies are more than diseconomies,RTS are increasing.
2. When economies are less than diseconomies, RTS are decreasing.
3. When economies are equal to diseconomies,RTS are constant

Economies & Diseconomies of Scale:-

Economies of Scale:- Economies are the benefits that the firms & industry get during the production process .These economies can be in terms of infrastructure,factors availability,raw materials,credit facilities etc.

Types:Economies are of two types as under

Economies

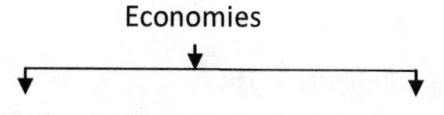

!) Internal Economies   ii)   External Economies

!) **Internal Economies** :-These are benefits derived by firms within the industry during the production process. They include a.Labour economies;-It means if the firms are able to get the productive, skilled & experienced labour.

b.Managerial economies;-It means if the firm is able to hire the talented, expert & experienced managers.

c.Purchase economies:-It means if the firm is able to purchase in bulk & concession from such purchases.

d.Raw material economies:-It means if the firm has access to the raw material which should be available.

e.Risk economies:-It means if the firm is able to undertake more & more risk.

f.Credit economies;-If the firm has reputation,good worth & able to get the credit.

ii.**External economies**:-These are the benefits derived by the industry during the production process. These are as under:

a. Transport Infrastructure economies: It means when there are well developed roads, railways,airways,availability of water, power supply etc.

b.Communication economies: It means well developed telephone, mobile, internet ,email, fax services & related infrastructure.

c.Specilisation by process: That is dividing the production process by specializing in one as in car industry some firms deal with machinery, some with body parts, some spare parts, some painting & so on.

d.Concentration:That localization of different industries near to one another which reduces time & transport costs.

e.Right budget policy: The right tax, expenditure policy also benefits the industry.

B.**Diseconomies**:-These are the handicaps & losses suffered by the firms & the industry during the production process.

Types of Diseconomies: These are of two types:

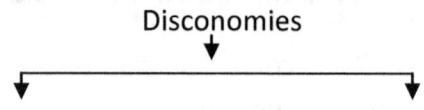

Disconomies

!) Internal Diseconomies   ii) External Diseconomies

!) **Internal diseconomies**: -These are losses suffered by the firms within the industry during the production process. They include

a.Labour diseconomies;-It means if the firms are not able to get the productive, skilled & experienced labour.

b.Managerial diseconomies;-It means if the firm is not able to hire the talented, expert & experienced managers.

c.Purchase diseconomies:-It means if the firm is not able to purchase in bulk & get no concession from such purchases.

d.Raw material diseconomies:-It means if the firm has no access to the raw material which which may be not available.

e.Risk diseconomies:-It means if the firm is not able to undertake more & more risk.

f.Credit diseconomies;-If the firm has no reputation no, good worth & not able to get the credit.

ii.**External diseconomies**:-These are the losses suffered by the industry during the production process. These are as under:

a. Transport Infrastructure diseconomies: It means when there are no well developed roads, railways,airways,availability of water, power supply etc.

b.Communication diseconomies: It means lack of developed telephone, mobile, internet ,email, fax services & related infrastructure.

c. No Specialization by process: That is lack of specialization.

d.No Concentration: That localization of different industries distant apart to one another which increases time & transport costs.

e.Unfavourable budget policy: The lack right tax, expenditure policy also makes the industry to suffer.

Homogeneous & Linear Production Function: A function $f(x)$ is said to be homogeneous of degree 'n' if by introducing a constant parameter λ replacing the variable x with λx we find

$$f(\lambda x) = \lambda^n f(x).$$

This function can be generalized to functions of more than two variables. For example, a function of more than two variables f(x,y) is said to be homogeneous of degree 'n' if

$$f(\lambda x, \lambda y) = \lambda^n f(x,y).$$

For example, the function $f(x,y) = 2x^2 - 3y2 + 4xy$ is a function of homogeneous of degree 2 because . $f(\lambda x, \lambda y) = 2(\lambda x)^2 - 3(\lambda y)^2 + 4(\lambda x)(\lambda y)$

$$f \qquad (\lambda x, \lambda y) = 2\lambda^2 x^2 - 3\lambda^2 y^2 + 4\lambda^2 xy$$

$$f(\lambda x, \lambda y) = \lambda^2(2x^2 - 3y2 + 4xy)$$

$$f(\lambda x, \lambda y) = \lambda^2 f(x,y)$$

Thus a production function is said to be homogeneous of degree n if any positive factor multiplying the inputs gives the output multiplied by the same factor.

Linear production function:A production function is said to be linear if it is a polynomial of dgree zero or one.When the function is only of one variable, it is of form f(x)=ax+b; where a & b are constants & x is the variable.

For a function f(x1,x2,.........xk) of any finite number of independent variables , the general formula for a linear function is f(x1,x2,.........xk) =b+a1x1+a2x2+a3x3+......+akxk where a1,a2,...ak,b are constants & x1,x2,...xk are variables'.

For example Cobb-Douglas Production function is of homogeneous degree one. It means if inputs are doubled, output will be be double & this indicates constant returns to scale. This can be written as

(Q)=f(L,K), here Q is the output & is function of inputs L & K ,IF L & K are multiplied by a factor ⋏, then output is also multiplied by the same factor ⋏ as:

⋏ (Q)=f(⋏ L, ⋏ K).This indicates constant RTS as if inputs are doubled ,output is also doubled as shown in the figure below:

Fig.2.16(a):Constant RTS

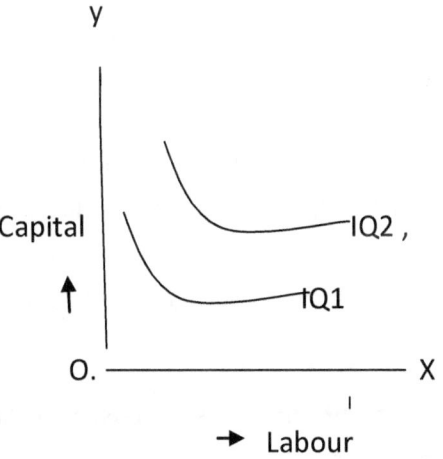

Here Q2=2Q1,i.e. as labour & capital is doubled, output is doubled so IQ2 is twice the IQ1 .

Cost of Production & concepts:-When there is demand, there will be supply, when there is supply ,there will be cost.Thus cost is the production expenditure.So cost is production cost in peoducing goods & services.

Cost

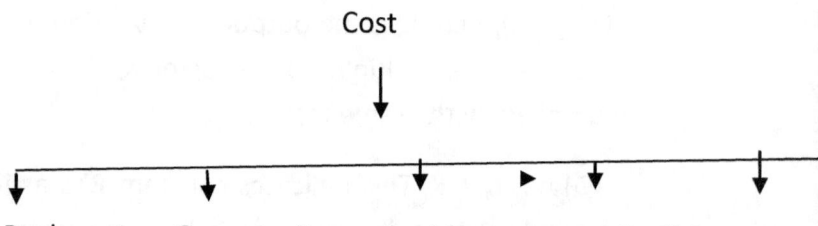

Real cost   Opportunity cost   Money cost   Explicit cost
Implicit cost

Private cost External cost Social

1.**Real cost**:-It means toil ,efforts, sacrifice,hardship,trouble & sweating undergone during the production process.

2.**Opportunity cost**:-It means opportunity lost,opportunity sacrificed.For instance if the consumer has Rs40 & he has two options as to buy icecream or pen each for Rs40.If he/she buys ice-cream then opportunity cost office-cream is the pen lost.

3.**Explicit cost**:-It is thecost of hiring factor services as land, labour, capital etc.

4.**Implicit cost**:It is the assumedcost of self owned factors of production as land, labour, capital etc.

5.**Private cost**:-It is the cost borne by the firm in producing goods & services.

6.**External cost**:-It is the cost borne by the society as the illness due to polluted air ,water as a result of industrialization

7.**Social Cost**= Private cost + External cost

8.**Economic COST**=Explicit +Implicit cost

9.**Accounting cos**t:-In accounting explicit costs are ignored, only implicit are considered, known as accounting cost.

10.**Money cost:**-It includes monetary expenditure during production process. It is most important analysis & has three aspects as

I.**Total cost (TC)**:-It is the total cost of production & has two components in the short run, i.e. fixed & variable as in the short run some factors are fixed & other are variable.Thus

TC=TFC+TVC

(A).**TFC(Total Fixed Cost)**:-It is the cost on fixed factors of production in the short run & does not change with the change in the output.e.g. rent,of building, wages of permanent employees.

TFC can be illustrated with the help of table & diagram as under:

Table 2.3:-TFC

Units of output	TFC
1	Rs100
2	Rs100
3	Rs100
4	Rs100
5	Rs100

The table 2.3 shows that even the ouput is rising but the FC remains same that is Rs100 & does not change.

Graphical presentation:-In figure output is along ox-axix & FC along oy-axis,the FC curve is parallel to ox-axis .

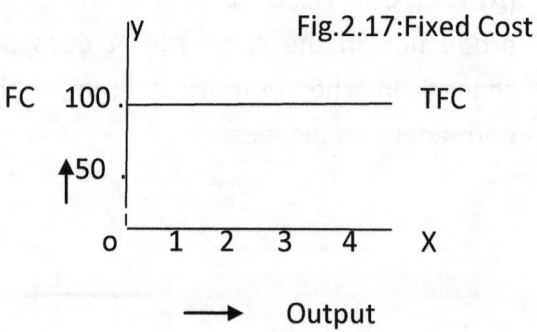

Fig.2.17:Fixed Cost

Average Fixed Cost(AFC):-AFC is the fixed cost per unit output & can be calculated as

AFC=TFC/N, Where N is no. of units of output.

AFC can be illustrated with the help of table & diagram as under:

Table 2.4:-AFC

Units of output	TFC	AFC
1	Rs100	Rs100
2	Rs100	Rs50
3	Rs100	RS33.3
4	Rs100	Rs25
5	Rs100	Rs20

The table 2.4   shows as the output is increasing, the FC remains the same but the AFC falls .

Graphical presentation:-In figure output is along ox-axix & AFC along oy-axis,the AFC curve is falling but does not touch to to ox-axis ,indicating that some fixed cost will always be there in the short run. .

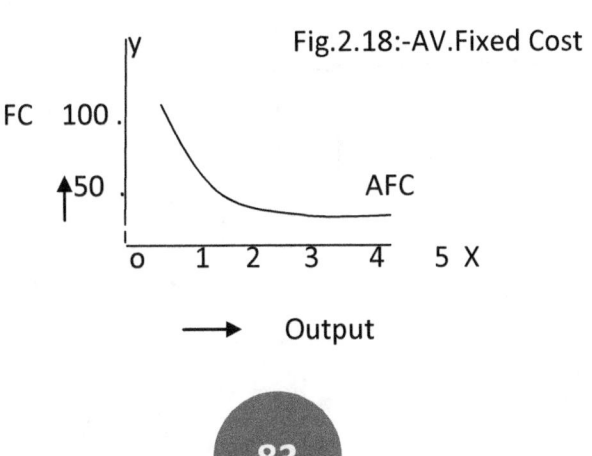

Fig.2.18:-AV.Fixed Cost

(B)**TVC(Total variable cost):-**It is the cost on variabl factors & it changes with the change in output.It includes daily wage labour cost, raw matial cost etc.

TVC can be illustrated with the help of table & diagram as under:-

Table 2.5:-TVC

Units of output	TVC
1	Rs10
2	Rs18
3	Rs28
4	Rs52
5	Rs80

The table shows as the output is changing, TVC is also changing.

Graphical presentation:-In figure 2.19, output is along ox-axix & TVC along oy-axis,the TVC curve is rising .

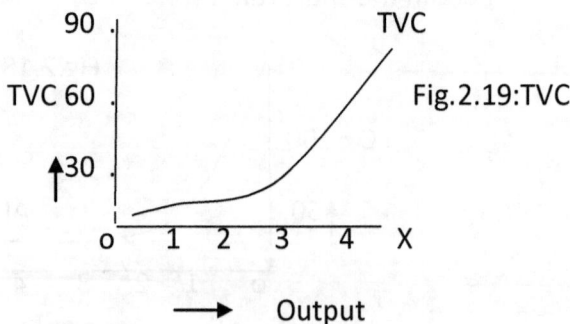

Fig.2.19:TVC

Average Variable Cost(AVC):-It is the variable cost per unit of the unit & can be calculated as

AVC=TVC/N,Where N is no. of units of output.

TVC can be illustrated with the help of table & diagram as under:-

Table 2.6:-TVC

Units of output	TVC	AVC
1	Rs10	Rs10
2	Rs18	Rs9
3	Rs28	Rs9.3
4	Rs52	Rs13
5	Rs80	Rs16

The table 2.6 shows as the output is rising, AVC is first falling ,then rising giving it U-shape.

Graphical presentation:- The figure 2.20, shows U-shaped AVC i.e. AVC first falls, the rises with the rising output.

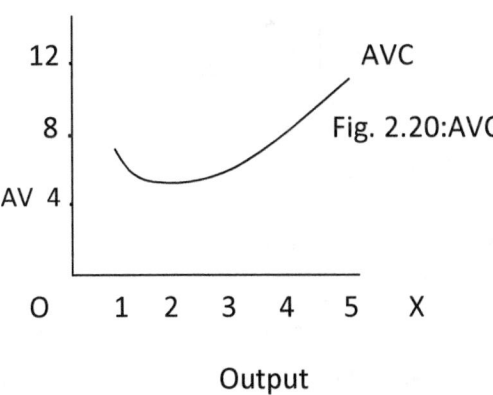

Fig. 2.20:AVC

Output

(II)**Av. Cost(AC):**-Av. Cost is the per unit cost & can be calculated as TC divided by no. of units of output,.ie.
AVC=   TC/N

Where N is the no. ofunits of output.

(III)**Marginal Cost(MC):**-It is the additional cost due the additional unit ofoutput produced & obtained by as change in total cost divided by the change in the number, i.e.

. $$MC= \Delta TC/\Delta N$$

Where ΔTC is the change in TC, ΔN is the change in no. of units of output.

Table 2.6:Relation between TC,AC & MC:-Short Run

Units of output	FC	VC	TC	AC	MC
0	Rs8	Rs0	10	∞	∞
1	Rs8	Rs10	18	18	8
2	Rs8	Rs16	24	12	6
3	Rs8	Rs25	33	11	9
4	Rs8	Rs44	52	13	19

In the table 2.6

1. 1st column shows output, 2nd FC, 3RD VC,4TH TC,5TH AC & 6TH MC.
2. Even at zero output FC is Rs 8, VC is Rs0,TC is Rs8+Rs0=Rs10,AC is ∞,Rs10 & so on as the output is

increasing, TC is changing with FC remaining fixed & VC changing.
3. From TC,AC,MC have been calculated as shown.
4. Firstly both AC & MC are falling but MC falls rapidly, then AC, MC rise ,but MC rising faster making inverted U-trend as in diagram.

Graphical presentation:-TC,AC & MC relationship can be shown graphically as under

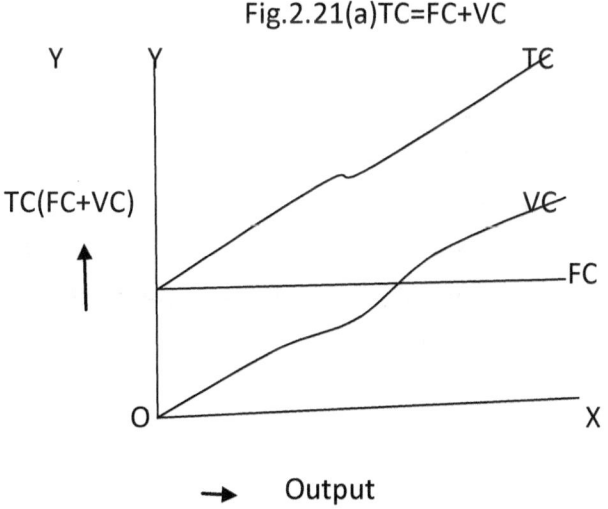

Fig.2.21(a)TC=FC+VC

In figure 2.21(a) ,TC curve is the sum of FC & VC curves, TC curve starts from   oy-axis not origin because there are fixed costs in the short run.

Fig.2.21(b) AC & MC

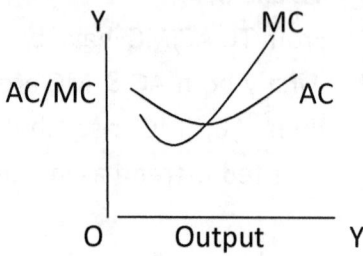

In figure 2.21(b) AC& MC curves are intersecting each other as

- When AC,MC both fall ,MC falls faster.
- MC cuts AC from below at minimum point o f AC.
- When both rise,MC rises faster.
  Thus AC,MC   are U-shaped because of the Law of Variable Proportions where AP, MP are inverted-U shaped.

Long Run TC,AC & MC:-In the long run, i.e. LTC starts from the origin because there are no fixed costs.LAC,LMC are U-shaped but more flatter than short run AC,MC ,because in the long run Returns to Scale is responsible for U-shape as shown the figures below:-

Graphical presentation:-Long run, .i.e.LTC,LAC &L MC relationship can be shown graphically as under

Fig.2.22(a)LTC

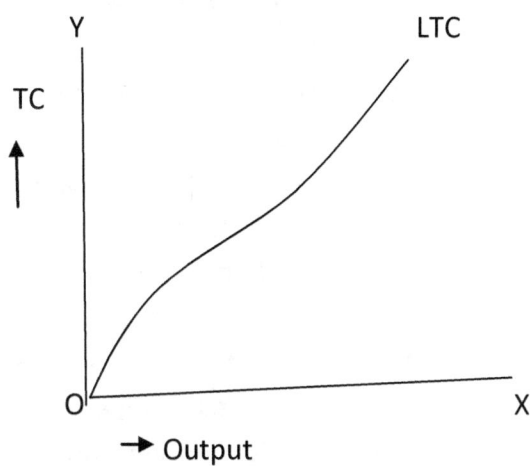

Fig.2.22(b) LAC &L MC

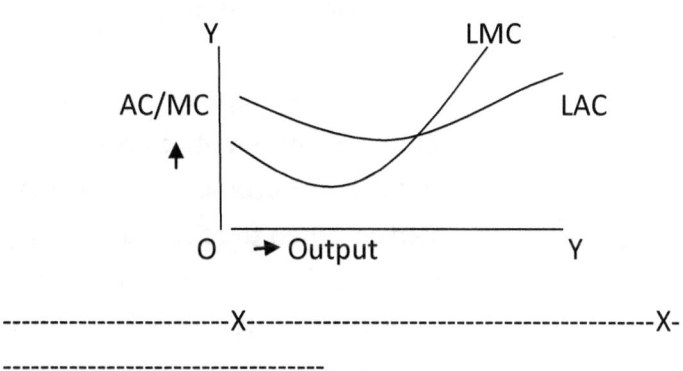

----------------------------X---X-

UNIT III   Market Structure

Tits-bits

Market: A place where goods & services are exchanged.

Perfect Market: A market where buyers & sellers are large, price is same ,products are identical, knowledge is perfect, transport cost is zero.

Pure Market: A market where buyers & sellers are large, price is same, products are identical.

Monopoly: The market where the seller is single.

Monopsony: It means there is only single buyer or the buyers act as a single group.

Monopolistic Competition: It is the mix market having both competitive & monopoly elements.

Price discrimination: The act of charging two different prices for the same good.

Dumping: It is the price discrimination at the international level.

Oligopoly: The market where there are few sellers only.

Price Leadership: When the dominant, aggressive, old or the barometric firm assumes the leadership & the others become the followers.

Cartel: When the firms under oligopoly join hands to set the price-output policy to maximize their profits.

Excess capacity: The gap between the potential output & the actual output.

TR, AR, MR: TR is the total revenue ,i.e the income from the sale of all the units of a good.AR is the average revenue calculated as AR=TR/n, where n is the number of units.MR is the revenue due to the additional unit sold & calculated as MR=ΔTR/Δn, where Δ is change.

Equilibrum point:The attains the equilibrium when MC=MR & MC is rising.In the short run the firm may earn abnormal profits, normal profits or even suffer losses but in the long run the firm earn normal or the abnormal profits only.

Markets:-

Meaning:-The market deals with the transaction of good & services.It is a place where buyers & sellers meet to exchange the goods & services at the agreed prices.The market place can be local, regional ,national or international.It can be with homogenous goods & services known as the perfect market & with different or unique goods & services the market is imperfect.

Types:-Market can be of two types:

I).Perfect Market II).Imperfect Market

I).**Perfect Market**:-

Meaning :-The market is said to be perfect if the number of buyers & sellers is large, price is uniform, products are homogeneous,knowledge among the buyers & sellers is perfect ,entry & exit for the firms is free in the long run.

Features/Characteristics:-The features of the perfect market also known as perfect completion are as under:

1.Large number of buyers & sellers:-In the perfect market the number o buyers & sellers is large there is competition among both for buying & selling.

2.Products are homogeneous:-The products in the perfect market are identical & perfect substitute for each other.In the eyes of the consumers products are homogeneous.

3.Price is uniform & given:-In the perfect market ,the price is determined by the supply & demand in the market or industry, hence for individual firms the price is given.Thus firm under

Perfect competition is the price taker not the price maker.

4.Knowledge is perfect:-Both the buyers & sellers have full knowledge of the market.The buyers are assumed to know the variety, price, availability of the goods & services & the sellers know the variety demanded,raw materials, prices etc.

5.Entry & exit is free:-In the long run the firms can enter the industry if it is profitable & the loss makers can exit the industry freely.

6.Demand is perfectly elastic:-Under the perfect competition ,the demand is perfectly elastic , hence the demand curve is parallel to ox-axis for the individual firm as shown in the figure 3.1.

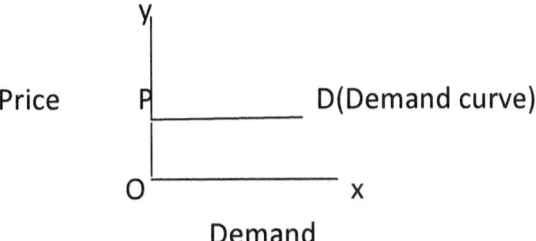

Fig.3.1:Demand curve for perferct competitive firm

7.No transport costs:-The transport costs are assumed to be zero taking into consideration that different firms within the industry are localized at zero distance.

8.No need for advertising costs:-It is assumed that firms will not incur advertising & selling costs because products are homogeneous & buyers have perfect knowledge of the market.

Equilibrium or Price-output policy under the perfect competition:-In the perfect market the firm has to adjust the output as the price is given.In the short run the firm may earn normal, supernormal profits or suffer losses but in the long run the firm earns normal profits only.Equilibrium is attained at a point.

Short Run Equilibrium:-

In the short run the firm may earn (a). normal,(b). supernormal profits or (c). suffer losses

a. Normal Profits:-In normal profits the AR=AC i.e. AR curve will be tangent to the AC curve as shown in fig.3.2(a):-

- Along ox-axis we have take output& along oy-axis we have taken price.
- AR,MR,AC&MC are average revenue, marginal revenue ,average cost & marginal cost respectively.
- E is the equilibrium point because MC=MR & MC cuts MR from below.
- OP is the equilibrium price & OQ is the equilibrium ouput corresponding to the point E.
- AR=AC,i.e. QE=QE,so profits are normal.

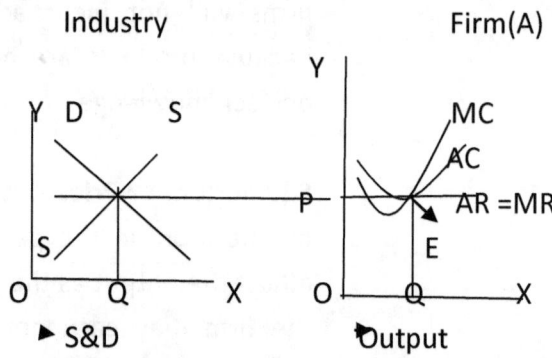

Industry   Firm(A)

Fig.3.2(a)Normal Profits

b. Abnormal Profits:-In abnormal profits the AR>AC i.e. AR curve will be below AC curve as shown in fig.3.2(b):-

- Along ox-axis we have take output& along oy-axis we have taken price.
- AR,MR,AC&MC are average revenue, marginal revenue ,average cost & marginal cost respectively.
- E is the equilibrium point because MC=MR & MC cuts MR from below.
- OP is the equilibrium price & OQ is the equilibrium ouput corresponding to the point E.

AR>AC,i.e. QE>QH,so profits are abnormal.Per unit profits are equal to EH & total profits=arPTEH.

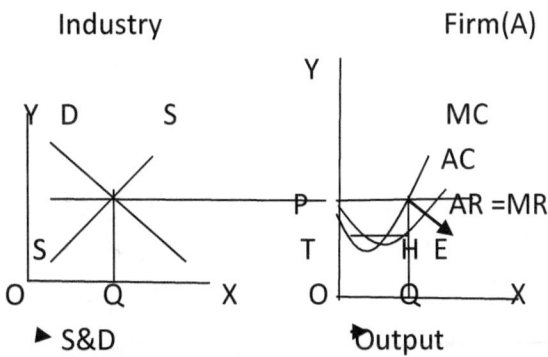

Fig.3.2(b)Abnormal Profits

c. Losses:-In losses the AR<AC i.e. AR curve will below the AC curve as shown in fig.3.2(c):-

- Along ox-axis we have take output& along oy-axis we have taken price.
- AR,MR,AC&MC are average revenue, marginal revenue ,average cost & marginal cost respectively.
- E is the equilibrium point because MC=MR & MC cuts MR from below.
- OP is the equilibrium price & OQ is the equilibrium output corresponding to the point E.

AR<AC, i.e. QE<QH,so the firm suffers losses. Per unit loss is equal to EH & total losses =arPTHE.

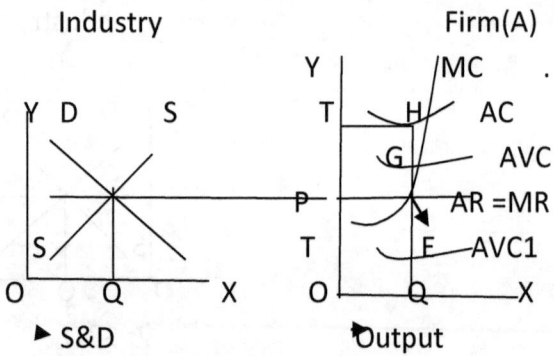

Industry   Firm(A)

Fig.3.2(c)Losses

Losses & shut down or continue:-During losses if we have to know whether firm will shut down or continue to operate, we assess AVC, if it is above price i.e.AR as in figure (c),AVC passes through point G, so G will be the shut down point. This is because after shut down ,loss is reduced from EH to GH as variable cost =QG will go & fixed cost=GH will remain. However, if the AVC is below AR, then firm will continue because shut down will increase the loss as AVC1 passes through point N.

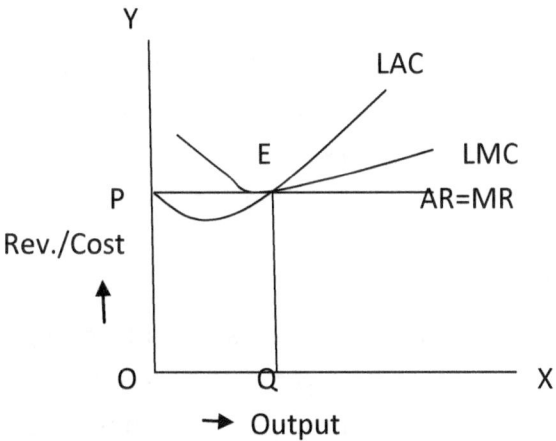

Fig.3.2(d): Long run normal profits

In the figure 3.2 (d

- Along ox-axis we have take output& along oy-axis we have taken price.
- LAC ,LMC,LAR,LMR are long run average cost, marginal cost ,average revenue & marginal revenue respectively.
- E is the equilibrium point because MC=MR & MC cuts MR from below.

- OP is the equilibrium price & OQ is the equilibrium output corresponding to the point E.

AR=AC,i.e. QE=QE,so profits are normal & can be written as

$$MC=MR=Min.LAC$$

Why Normal Profits only? The normal profits in the LR are because of free entry & exit ,i.e. new firm lured by the profits in the short run enter the industry , increase the supply, price falls & thus profits fall to normal the where as the loss making firms either improve or leave the industry in the LR.

The equilibrium of the firm in the long run is the equilibrium of the industry.

(B)The Imperfect Market:- The market is said to be imperfect if the number of buyers & sellers is not large, price is not uniform, products are not homogeneous, knowledge among the buyers & sellers is not perfect ,entry & exit for the firms is not free in the long run.It includes   Monopoly, duopoly,oligopoly,monopolistic ,competition,monopsony etc.

I.Monoply,Meaning & Features:

Meaning:-Mono means single & poly means seller, so monopoly is a market in which there is a single seller in the the market.

Features/Characteristics:-The features of the Monopoly market also known as single seller market are as under:

1.Single seller & many buyers:-In the monopoly there is only one & single seller but the number of the buyers is many.

2.Products are unique:-The products in the monopoly market are of unique type & have no close substitute..In the eyes of the consumers products are of unique type as gas cylinders, envelops of post-office.

3.Price output control:-In the monopoly ,the price-output policy is under the full control of monopoly firm, hence for the monopolist firms the price makers.

4.Knowledge is not perfect:-Both the buyers & sellers lack full knowledge of the market. The buyers lack awareness about the variety, price, availability of the goods & services & the sellers also do not know the variety demanded, raw materials, prices etc.

5.Entry & exit is not free:-In the long run the firms can enter the industry   if it is profitable & the loss makers can exit the industry freely in the competitive market but under monopoly there are barriers to entry & exit.

6.Demand is relatively inelastic:-Under the perfect competition ,the demand is perfectly elastic , hence the demand curve is parallel to ox-axis for the individual firm but under monopoly demand curve is downward sloping as shown in the figures 3.3(a) &(b) respectively:

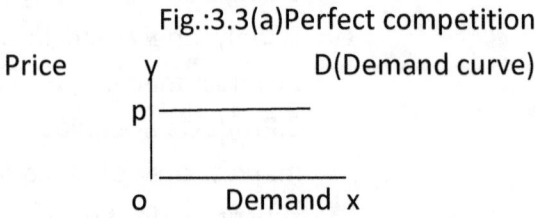

Fig.:3.3(a)Perfect competition

Price   y   D(Demand curve)

p

O   Demand x

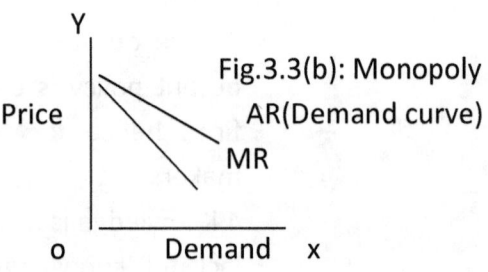

Y

Fig.3.3(b): Monopoly

Price   AR(Demand curve)

MR

O   Demand   x

7.Transport costs considered:-The transport costs are taken into consideration in the price ouput policy.

8.No need for advertising costs:-It is assumed that firms will not incur advertising & selling costs because products are of unique type.

9.No difference between the firm & the industry:-In monopoly the firm & the industry are treated as one,i.e. firm is the industry, industry is the firm.

10.Price discrimination possible:-Monopoly has thepower to discriminate or charge different prices from the buyers.

Equilibrium or Price-output policy under the Monopoly:-In the Monopoly market, the firm has to price-output at its own because of monopoly power.In the short run the firm may earn normal, supernormal profits or suffer losses but in the long lun the firm earns normal or abnormal profits .Equilibrium is attained at a point where MC=MR & MC cuts MR from below.

Short Run Equilibrium:-

In the short run the firm may earn (a). normal,(b). supernormal profits or (c). suffer losses

a.Normal Profits:-In normal profits the AR=AC i.e. AR curve will be tangent to the AC curve as shown in fig.3.4(a):-

- Along ox-axis we have take output& along oy-axis we have taken price.
- AR,MR,AC&MC are average revenue, marginal revenue ,average cost & marginal cost respectively.
- E is the equilibrium point because MC=MR & MC cuts MR from below.

- OP is the equilibrium price & OQ is the equilibrium ouput corresponding to the point E.

- AR=AC,i.e. QE=QE,so profits are normal.

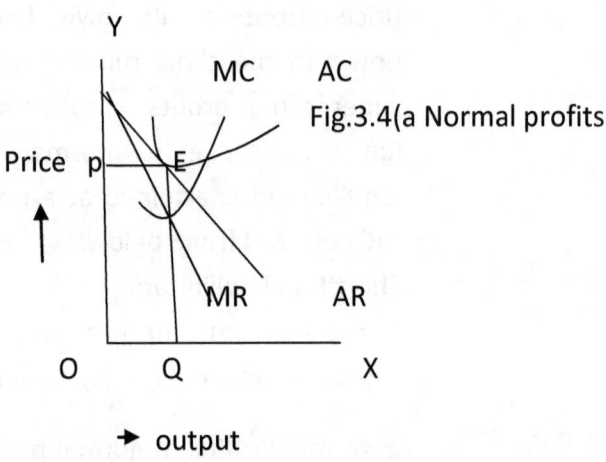

Fig.3.4(a Normal profits

→ output

b.abnormal Profits:-In abnormal profits the AR>AC i.e. AR curve will be below AC curve as shown in fig.3.4(b):-

- Along ox-axis we have take output& along oy-axis we have taken price.
- AR,MR,AC&MC are   average revenue, marginal revenue ,average cost & marginal cost respectively.
- E is the equilibrium point because MC=MR & MC cuts MR from below.
- OP is the equilibrium price & OQ is the equilibrium ouput corresponding to the point E.

AR>AC,i.e.   QH>QN,so   profits   are abnormal.Per unit profits are equal to NH & total profits=arPTNH.

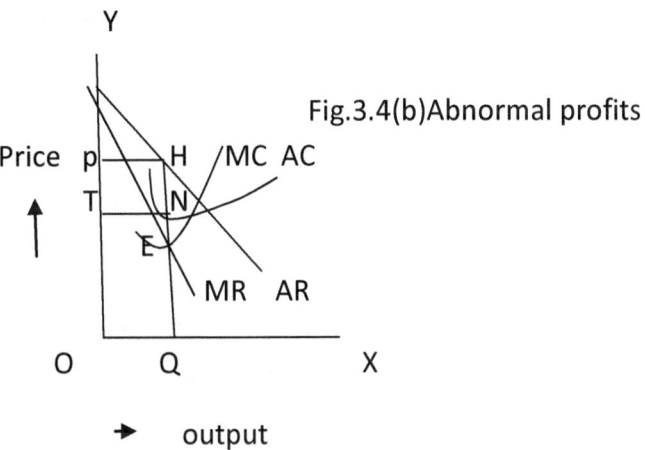

Fig.3.4(b)Abnormal profits

c.Losses:-In losses the AR<AC i.e. AR curve will below the AC curve as shown in fig3.4(c):-

- Along ox-axis we have take output& along oy-axis we have taken price.
- AR,MR,AC&MC   are   average   revenue, marginal revenue ,average cost & marginal cost respectively.
- E is the equilibrium point because MC=MR & MC cuts MR from below.

- OP is the equilibrium price & OQ is the equilibrium ouput corresponding to the point E.

    AR<AC,i.e. QE<QH,so the firm suffers losses.Per unit loss is equal to EH & total losses =arPTNH.

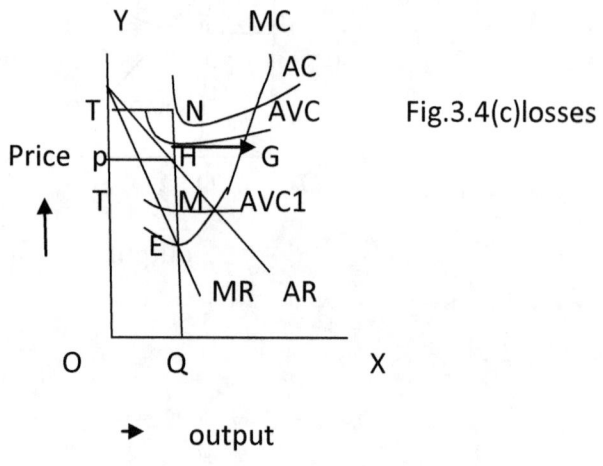

Fig.3.4(c)losses

→ output

Losses & shut down or continue:-During losses if we have to know whether firm will shut down or continue to operate, we assess AVC, if it is above price i.e.AR as in figure 3.4(c),AVC passes through point G, so G will be the shut down point.This is because after shut down ,loss is reduced from NH to GH as variable cost =QG will go & fixed cost=GH will remain.However, if the AVC is below AR, then firm will continue because shut down will increase the loss as AVC1 psses through point M.

Long run Equilibrium under monopoly:-

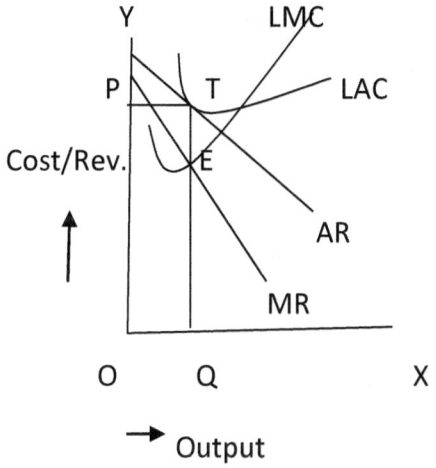

Fig.3.4(d)NormalProfits

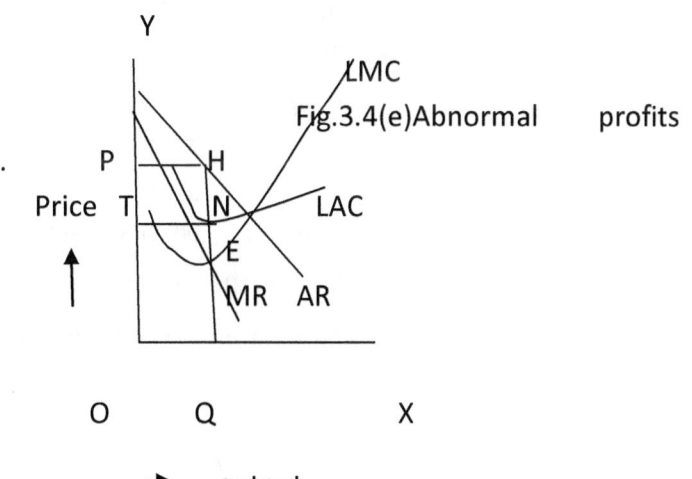

Fig.3.4(e)Abnormal profits

In figure 3.4(d), the firm earning LR profits along ox-axis we have take output& along oy-axis we have taken price.

- LAR,LMR,LAC&LMC are long run average revenue, marginal revenue ,average cost & marginal cost respectively.
- E is the equilibrium point becauseL MC=LMR & MC cuts MR from below.
- OP is the equilibrium price & OQ is the equilibrium ouput corresponding to the point E.

AR=AC,i.e. QE=QE,so profits are normal.

In figure 3.4(e) Along ox-axis we have take output& along oy-axis we have taken price.

- LAR,LMR,LAC&LMC are long run average revenue, marginal revenue ,average cost & marginal cost respectively.
- E is the equilibrium point because LMC=LMR & MC cuts MR from below.
- OP is the equilibrium price & OQ is the equilibrium ouput corresponding to the point E.

  AR>AC,i.e. QH>QN,so profits are abnormal.Per unit profits are equal to NH & total profits=arPTNH.

II.Monopolistic competition:-,Meaning & Feature:

Meaning:-Monopolistic competition means blend of monopoly & competition,.i.e. the market where the firms have monopoly power but also face the competition from the other firms in the market. This type of market is between the two extremes i.e monopoly & the perfect competition(which are rare) & is more realistic worked out by Sir Chamberlin in 1853.

Features/Characteristics:-The features of the Monopolistic competitive market are as under:-

1.Many sellesr & many buyers:-In the monopolistic competition there are many sellers & many buyers.The number is between the perfect competition & the monopoly.

2.Products aredifferentiated:-The products in the monopolistic competition are diffentiated & have close substitutes as pepsodent paste for coalgate paste.The products differentiation can be price based or non-price based as design, quality, advertising ,sale dealing,credit facility,shopping comforts etc.

3.Price output control partial:-In the monoploy ,the price-output policy is under the full control of monopoly firm, but under monopolistic competition the control is partial because there is monopoly power but rivals have to be faced while pricing goods & services.

4.Knowledge is not perfect:-Both the buyers & sellers lack full knowledge of the market. The buyers lack awareness about the variety, price, availability of the goods & services & the sellers also do not know the variety demanded, raw materials, prices etc.

5.Entry & exit is not completely free:-In the long run the firms can enter the industry if it is profitable & the loss makers can exit the industry freely in the competitive market but under monopoly there are barriers to entry & exit. However under monopolistic competition there is middle position

6.Demand is relatively elastic:-Under the perfect competition ,the demand is perfectly elastic , hence the demand curve is parallel to ox-axis for the individual firming but under monopoly demand curve is downward sloping under monopolistic competition , the demand curve is downward sloping but more elastic than monopoly & less than perfect market as shown in the figures 3.5(a),(b) & (c):

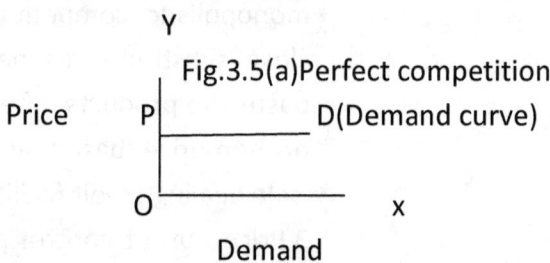

Fig.3.5(a)Perfect competition

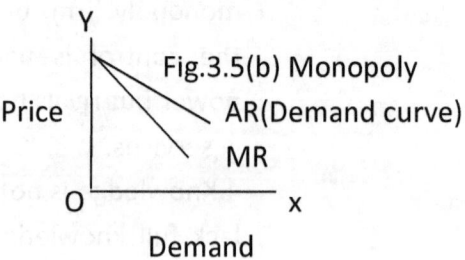

Fig.3.5(b) Monopoly

Fig.(3.5c):
Monopolistic Competition

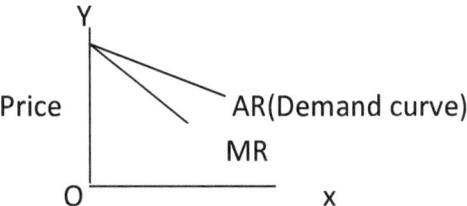

7.Transport costs considered:-The transport costs are taken into consideration in the price ouput policy.

8.Urgent need for advertising costs:-In this market firms will incur heavy advertising & selling costs because because without this survival in the market becomes difficult.

9.Firms together called as Group not the industry:-In monopolistic competition y there is Group behavior, i.e group of all the firms as firms are rival, even though the industrial group is one ,.eg. soap industry where firms produce different brands.

10.Long run equilibrium:-In theshort run the firm may earn normal, abnormal profits or even suffer losses but in thelong run the Group is characterized by the Execess Capacity.

Equilibrium or Price-output policy under theMonopolistic competition:-In the short run run the firm may earn normal, supernormal profits or suffer losses.Equilibrium is attained at a point where MC=MR & MC cuts MR from below but in the LR the Group is characterized by the Excess capacity(E.C) because of entry & exit is not freely complete..

Short Run Equilibrium:-In the short run the firm may earn (a). normal,(b). supernormal profits or (c). suffer losses

a.Normal Profits:-In normal profits the AR=AC i.e. AR curve will be tangent to the AC curve as shown in fig.3.6(a):-Along ox-axis we have take output& along oy-axis we have taken price.

- AR,MR,AC&MC are average revenue, marginal revenue ,average cost & marginal cost respectively.
- E is the equilibrium point because MC=MR & MC cuts MR from below.
- OP is the equilibrium price & OQ is the equilibrium ouput corresponding to the point E.
- AR=AC,i.e. QH=QH,so profits are normal.

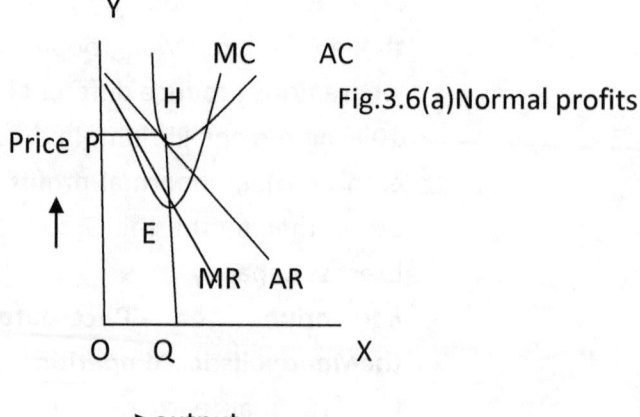

Fig.3.6(a)Normal profits

b.abnormal Profits:-In abnormal profits the AR>AC i.e. AR curve will be below AC curve as shown in fig.3.6(b):-

- Along ox-axis we have take output& along oy-axis we have taken price.
- AR,MR,AC&MC are average revenue, marginal revenue ,average cost & marginal cost respectively.
- E is the equilibrium point because MC=MR & MC cuts MR from below.
- OP is the equilibrium price & OQ is the equilibrium ouput corresponding to the point E.

    AR>AC,i.e.   QH>QN,so   profits   are abnormal.Per unit profits are equal to NH & total profits=arPTNH.

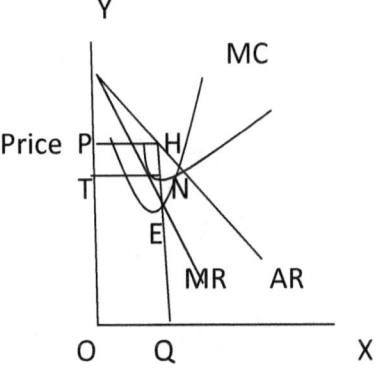

Fig.(3.6b):Abnormal Profits

c.Losses:-In losses the AR<AC i.e. AR curve will below the AC curve as shown in fig.3.6(c):-

- Along ox-axis we have take output& along oy-axis we have taken price.
- AR,MR,AC&MC are average revenue, marginal revenue ,average cost & marginal cost respectively.
- E is the equilibrium point because MC=MR & MC cuts MR from below.
- OP is the equilibrium price & OQ is the equilibrium ouput corresponding to the point E.

    AR<AC,i.e. QE<QH,so the firm suffers losses.Per unit loss is equal to EH & total losses =arPTNH.

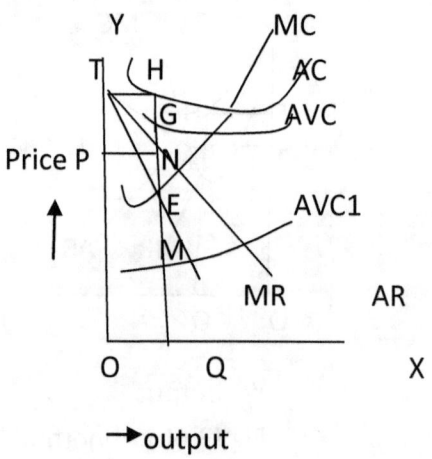

Losses & shut down or continue:-During losses if we have to know whether firm will shut down or continue to operate, we assess AVC, if it is above price i.e.AR as in figure 3.6(c),AVC passes through point G, so G will be the shut down point.This is because after shut down ,loss is reduced from NH to GH as variable cost =QG will go & fixed cost=GH will remain.However, if the AVC is below AR, then firm will continue because shut down will increase the loss as AVC1 psses through point M.

Long Run Equilibrium for the Group under Monopolistic Competition:-For the lon run equibrium two assumption have to be made:

1.Symmetry Assumption:Demand & cost curves for all the firms are same.

2.Heroic assumptions:Individual firm has to influence on other rivals in regard to price output behavior.

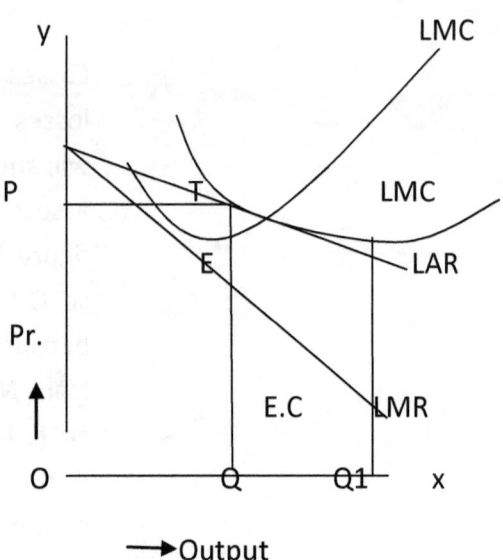

→Output

In figure(d), the firm earning LR profits along ox-axis we have take output& along oy-axis we have taken price.

- LAR,LMR,LAC&LMC are long run average revenue, marginal revenue ,average cost & marginal cost respectively.
- E is the equilibrium point becauseL MC=LMR & MC cuts MR from below.
- OP is the equilibrium price & OQ is the equilibrium ouput corresponding to the point E.

AR=AC,i.e. QE=QE,so profits are normal but the firm is producing (at falling portion of LAC not at its minimum point) less than the competitive output & charging more than the competitive price, so characterized by gap in output,i.e.QQ1, which could be avoided by producing at minimum point LAC at eqbm. Point E1.The gap between the actual & potential output is known as Excess Capacity(E.C).This is because of some barriers to the entry of new firms.

Oligopoly:-Meaning & Features:

Meaning:-Oligo means few & poly means seller, thus oligopoly is the market wherethe competition is amo ng the few firms.

Features:-

1.Competition among the few:-It is the market where the there are few sellers say 2-10 in the market as small car firms.

2. Homogenenous/Heterogeneous products:-The oligopoly with homogeneous products is called pure & oligopoly with different products is called heterogeneous oligopoly.

3. Price-output policy not determinate & interdependent:- For price-output policy the firms have to take rivals action – reaction into consideration which are uncertain, hence there is interdependence but because of uncertainty price-output strategy is not known..

4. Advertising & selling costs important:-These costs are the heart of the business for survival in the market.

5. Demand curve:-Because of unknown actions by the rivals demand curve is unknown.

6. Collusive/Non-collusive Oligopoly:-The oligopoly is collusive if the firms join the hands to maximize the profits & if it does not happen the oligopoly is non-collusive.

Equilibrium /Price-output policy:-As the price-output indeterminate, because demand curve is not known ,so there are certain models to solve the problem as under:-

1.**Price leadership model**:-According to Price leadership model one leads the others follow, so one

Firm assumes the leadership, others become the followers.

Types:-Price leadership is of following types:

I. **Leadership by a dominant firm**:-That is when a dominant firm with good market power assumes the leadership.

Assumptions:-

1. There is one dominant leader.
2. The other firms are small.3.The leader knows the supply & demand conditions of the small firms.

3.Leader`s Demand curve starts from where the the others firms meet the supply.

Explanation:-

Fig.3.7 Dominant Leadership

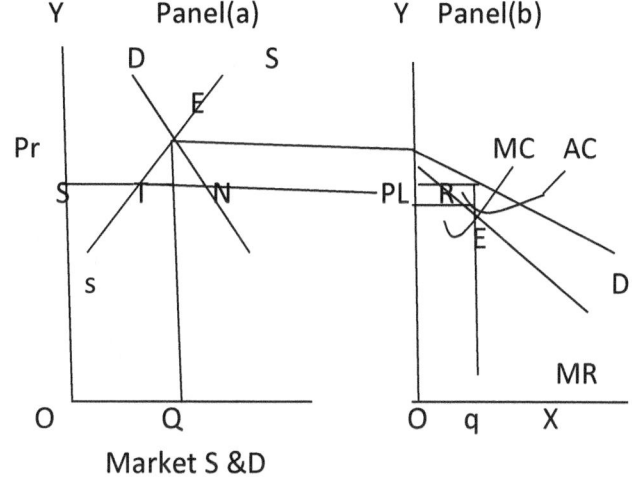

Market S &D

In figure ,panel(a), SS & DD are the supply Y demand curves of the market & E is the equilibrium point.Now the price leader in panel(b) sets the demand curve corresponding to equilibrium point, sets profit maximizing price as OPL.AC, M,AR,MRC curves reflect the equilibrium point at E & Profits as R,the rectangle.

The leader asks the firms to follow his price , thereby produce TN part of demand & keep ST =Oq for the leader.

II. **LEADERSHIP BY A LOW COST FIRM:**-In this type the low cost firm in the group assumes the leadership & the others fo follow the leader.

Assumptions:

1.There are two firms in the market A & B.

117

1.A is a high cost & B is a low cost, hence AC,MC of B will lie low.

3.Being low cost ,B will become the leader.

Explanation:-

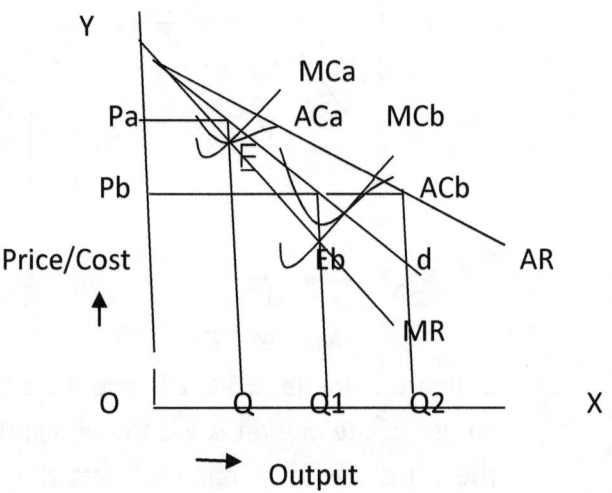

Fig.3.8 Price leadership by a dominant firm

In figure 3.8:-

1. Along ox-axis we have taken output & along oy-axis we have taken price & cost.

2.AR is the market demand curve & the firms A & B operate on the half demand curve d.Below the demand curve there is MR curve.

3. ACa, MCa are the cost curves of high cost firm & AC, MCb are the cost curves of the low cost firm which are at lower level.

4.E is the equilibrium of the high cost firm A & Eb is the equilibrium of the low cost firm B.Thus OPa is the price of the firm A & OPb is the price of firm B.

5.As the firm B is low cost so it becomes leader & the firm B has to follow by selling at OPb & producing OQ ,thus OQ+QQ1=OQ2(Total output).

III.**Leadership by Exploitative Firm**:-In this type the powerful firm with pressurizing & threatening others in the market becomes the leader.

IV.Leadership by a barometric firm:-In this type old & experienced firm working in the interests of all firms in the market becomes the leader.

2. **Kink-Demand curve/Sweezy Model**:-In 1939, P.Sweezy advocated the Kinked- Demand Curve Model. According to this model the Oligopoly faces kinked demand curve,i.e. a curve having two parts upper more elastic lower one less elastic indicating neither moving to rise nor towards fall in price is possible. So the price remains rigid or fixed at the point of Kink. Thus the model is also known as price rigidity model.

1. The oligopoly has Kinked-D curve.

2. The remains fixed at the point of kink.

Explanation:-

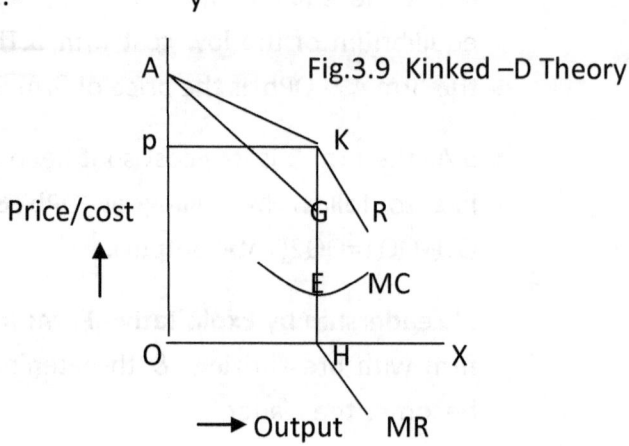

Fig.3.9 Kinked –D Theory

In figure 3.9:

1.Along ox-axis we have taken output & along oy-axis we have taken price & cost.

2.AR curve is kinked   at point K, thus AK part more elastic & KR part less elastic.

3. Below AR is MR which is also broken with gap GH.

4. MC passes through the gap GH, thus E is the equilibrium as MC=MR & MC is rising.

∴. OP is the equilibrium price& OQ is the equilibrium output. The price remains fixed because the firm cannot raise the price above OP as others will not follow the price rise, thus the price raiser fir will loose the customers & the firm cannot decrease the price below the OP because others will also follow the price cut. So there is no benefit to change the price for the firms.

Criticism:

1.The theory fails to determine the price −output because it has taken the price given & fixed.

2.What is the exact location of the kink ,the theory has no answer.

3.Price can never remain fixed.

4.Increase in demand can cause the price to rise by shifting the kink demand curve to right upward.

...........................#.....................#.............................

Unit IV   Factor Pricing

Tits-bits:

Factors of Production: Production is not possible without factor inputs, so there are four factors of production as land, labour, capital & the entrepreneur.

Land: It means resources upon the earth, soil & the resources beneath the earth. Its price is rent or royalty.

Capital: The part of the wealth used for further production is called capital. For the use of the capital, price paid is the interest.

Labour: the physical & mental services performed constitute the labour & for using the services of labour, the price paid is wage.

Entrepreneur: The organizer of other factors, the risk bearer & the business starter is the entrepreneur.

Factor prices: Prices paid to the factors as rent to the land, wages to the labour, interest to the capital & profits to the entrepreneur.

TRP, ARP, MRP: TRP is the total revenue product of the factor & obtained as TP×AR.ARP is the average revenue product & calculated as TRP/n, where n is the number of factor inputs say labour.MRP is marginal revenue product & is calculated as MP×MR.

MVP:It is the marginal value of the product & calculated as MRP, i.e.MVP=MP× MR.

Fertility differential: It means difference in fertility level of the soil or land.

Rent: It is surplus over & above the minimum supply price of natural factors.

Quasi-Rent: It is a short term surplus over & above the minimum supply price of the man made factors as machinery & tools.

Monopoly Profits: Profits due to monopoly power.

Uncertainty: Bearing the unknown risks which are not insurable as change in demand.

Innovation: Introducing something new as ideas, products, techniques, designs etc.

Factor Pricing

Theories on factor pricing: The factor pricing deals with the pricing of factors of production as land, labour, capital & entrepreneur. These prices are as rent for land, wages for labour, interest for capital & profits for the entrepreneurs. The question is how factors are paid or rewarded or priced.

Marginal Productivity Theory:-This theory was developed by J.B.Clark ,Henry Wicksteed & others.Acording to this theory , the factors of production are paid(called MFC, i.e. marginal factor cost) according to their marginal contributions(MP×Price=Marginal value of product,MVP) ,i.e. the factor price is equal to the MVP ,i.e. marginal value of the product.

MVP(MRP) & AVP(ARP):-ARP is the average revenue product obtained as AP×AR=ARP, where as MRP is obtained as MP×MR=MRP.Like AP & MP, ARP &ARP are inverted U-shaped as in the diagram below:

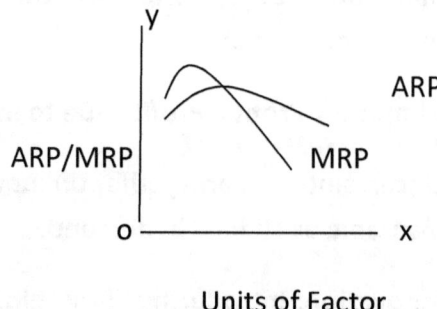

Fig.4.1 Marginal product

Explanation: The theory can be explained with the help of a table & diagram as under:

Table 4.1: Marginal Productivity Theory

Units of labour	MP	Price/kg	MVP	MFC
1	50kg	Rs10	Rs500	Rs300
2	40kg	Rs10	Rs400	Rs300
3	30kg	Rs10	Rs300	Rs300
4	20kg	Rs10	Rs200	Rs300

The table 4.1 shows as the units of labour employment increases, marginal value of the product goes on diminishing, price of the product is same ,i.e.Rs10 & price of the factor is also same ,i.e. Rs300.when the 3rd unit of labour is employed ,the firm attains the equilibrium, i.e. MVP=MFC, thus the factor price equals the factor`s contribution.

Explanation:-According to MRP, Theory the factors are paid equal to their marginal products as shown in the figure 4.2 below:

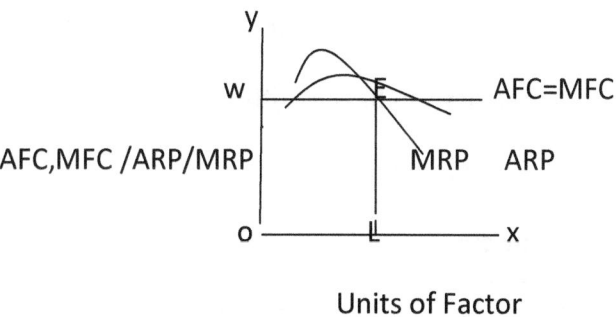

Fig.4.2 Marginal product equals Marginal wage

- Along ox-axis is the employment of factor say labour & along oy-axis factor cost & revenue from the product produced.
- AFC=MFC is average factor =marginal factor cost as AR=MR under perfect completion.
- ARP & MRP when both rise MRP rises faster & when both fall MRP falls faster, MRP cuts ARP at maximum from above.

- E is the equilibrium point because MFC=MRC & MRP cuts MFC from above.

∴ OL is the equilibrium factor employment & OW is the equilibrium factor price.

Assumptions:-

1. All factor inputs are homogenous.

2. There is perfect completion.

3. Factors can move from one occupation to another.

4. Factors can be substituted for each other.

5. There are diminishing marginal returns.

Criticism;-

1. All factor inputs cannot be homogenous because there can skill, training, educational & capability variations.

2. There is perfect completion in the real world economies.

3. Factors can move from one occupation to another but not so easy.

4. Factors cannot be substituted for each other so perfectly as assumed.

5. The use of technology can avoid the diminishing marginal returns.

Modern Theory of Factor Pricing:-According to modern theory the factor price is determined by the forces of supply & demand for the factors of production.

Demand for Factor:-The demand for goods & services is direct but the demand for factors is derived because it is derived by the goods & services we want. So the demand for factors is indirect or derived & follows the law of demand that is as the factor price rises , demand falls & vice versa as shown in the figure 4.3(a) below.

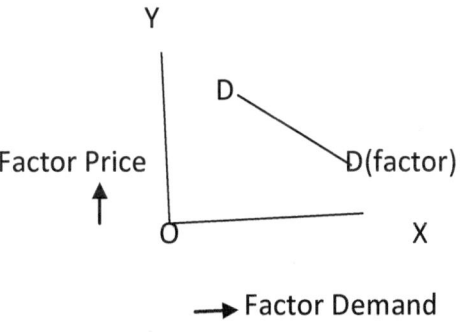

Fig.4.3(a) Factor demand

Supply of Factor:-Unlike the supply of goods & services ,supply of factors is complex as the law of supply may not always fit in factor supply case. For instance increasing wages may cause the labour to work less & enjoy leisure more, giving backward bending labour supply curve as shown in the figure 4.2(b) below:

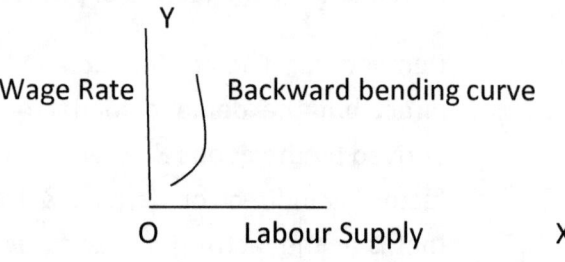

Fig.4.3(b) Factor supply

However for sake of simplicity, we have taken upward to right sloping supply curve of the factor as per the the law of supply as shown in the figure 4.3(c) below;

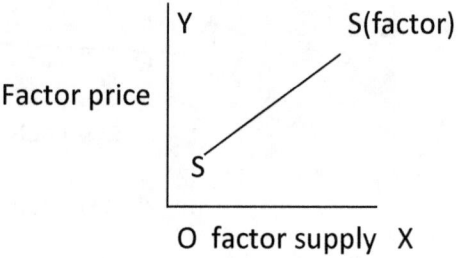

Fig.4.3(c) Factor supply

Equilibrium Factor Price:-The factor price is determined at a point where the supply of factor equals the demand for factor ,i.e. where the demand curve cuts the supply curve of factor as shown in the figure 4.3(d) below.

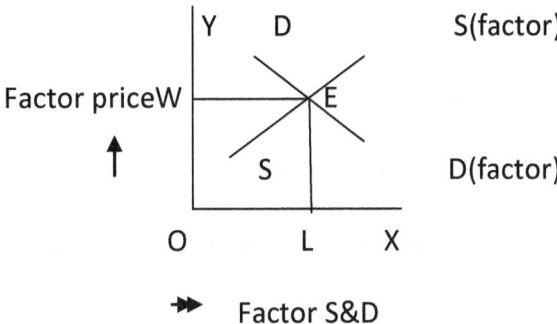

Fig.4.3(d) Equilibrium Factor price

In the figure E is the equilibrium point where SS curve cuts the DD curve ,so OW is the equilibrium factor price & OL is the factor quantity.

Recadian Rent Theory:-Sir Ricardo gave theory of rent & according to him rent arises to land only. He de fines rent as that portion of the produce which goes to the landlord for utilizing the services of land. According to him Rent arises on three accounts:

i.Fertility difference

ii.Situation difference

Iii.Land scarcity

Assumptions:-

1.Land is fixed in supply & has original powers of production & fertility.

2.Land differs in fertility.

3.Highly fertile land is cultivated first.

4.There is marginal or no rent land.

5.The theory is based on the law of diminishing returns.

Explanation:

i. Fertility   Rent:-This type of rent arises due to fertility difference as rent equal to yield from high fertile land minus yield from low fertile land as explained   diagrammatically under:-

a.Extensive cultivation:.In this type different types of land are cultivated according to fertility grades as shown in the figure4.4(a).

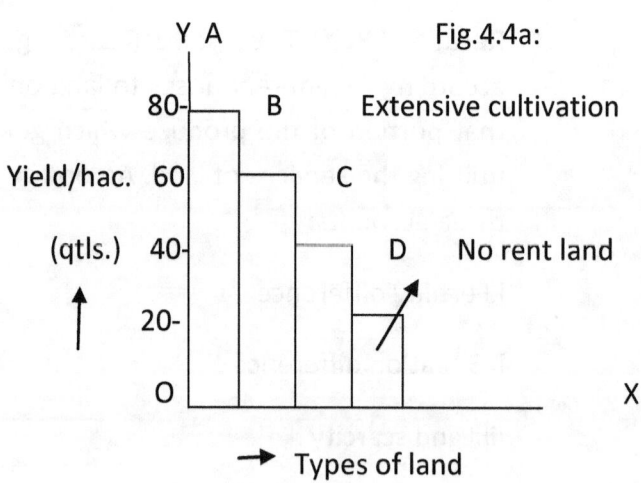

Fig.4.4a: Extensive cultivation

In figure along ox-axis are types of land as A,B,C,D wth Aas highly fertile & D as least fertile,along oy-axis is yield per hectare in quintals as yield from land A is 80qtls. & from D is 20qtls.

The 1ST people group moving to area for cultivation prefers land A being most fertile & there will be no question of renr because now A no rent land,next group moving to area will cultivate land B or land A, in both cases there will be rent for land A because if A is cultivated ,1st group will ask for rent equal to 20qtls,if freely available land B is cultivated there will rent because market price of wheat will be on the basis of cost of land B.

Again if 3rd group goes ,it can cultivate A,B or freely available C land, here C is no rent land but both A & B earn rent & so on for land D which yield no rent & called no rent or marginal land. Rent calculation has been shown in the table as under:

Table:-Rent calculation

Type of land	Yield from most fertile land	Yield from no rent land	Rent
A	80QTLS.	20QTLS	60QTLS
B	60QTLS.	20QTLS	40QTLS
C	40QTLS.	20QTLS	20QTLS.
D	20QTLS	20QTLS	0QTLS

No rent/Marginal land

b.Intensive cultivation:-In this cultivation the plot is same but we are applying doses of capital & labor with 1st dose most productive & last as marginal or no rent dose as shown in the fig.4.4(b)

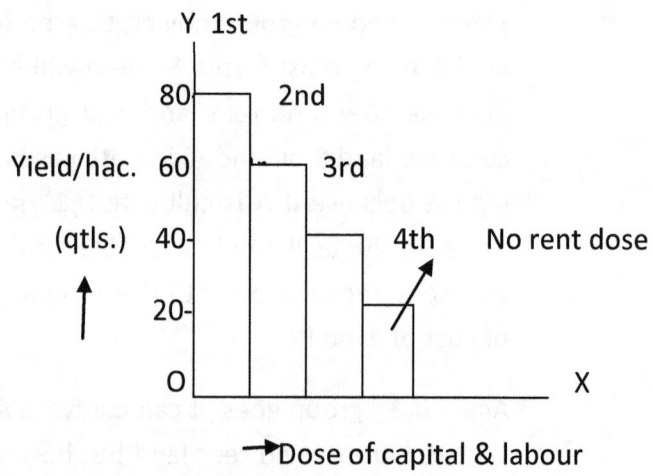

Fig4.4(b):Intensive Cultivation

In figure 4.4 (b) rent cultivation is same as superior dose minus inferior dose as show in the table below:

Table:-Rent calculation

Type of land	Yield from most productive dose	Yield from no rent dose	Rent
A	80QTLS.	20QTLS	60QTLS
B	60QTLS.	20QTLS	40QTLS
C	40QTLS.	20QTLS	20QTLS.
D	20QTLS	20QTLS	0 QTLS

No rent/Marginal dose

ii.Situational Rent:According to Sir Recardo rent also arises due situation of land as favourably situated land near to cities & roadside earns more rent or costs more than the land situated less favourably.

iii.Scarcity Rent:-According to this concept land supply is fixed but the demand is more so rent arises when demand exceeds supply as shown in the figure below:-In figure 4.5, when demand is dd, there is no rent, when demand for land is D1D1 , there is no rent but when demand exceeds as shown by D2D2, supply being fixed as SS curve showing fixed supply, as the demand is exceeding the supply at equilibrium point E, so OR is the rent.

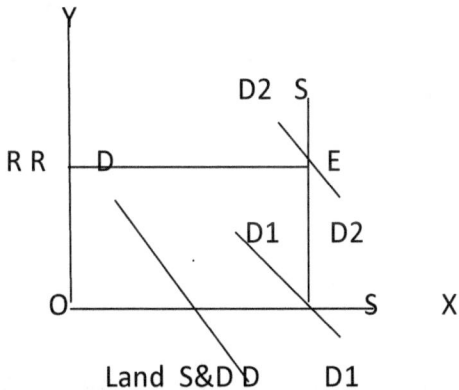

Fig.4.5 Scarcity Rent

Criticism:-

1. Land has no original & indestructible powers.
2. There is no marginal or no rent land.
3. It is not true that land will always be cultivated in decreasing fertility order.

   Quasi-Rent:-This concept was given by Sir Marshal.According to this concept rent arises not only due to land scarcity but also other scarce factors which are manmade as tools & machinery in the short run.For instance if during war time or emergency there is shortage of machinery, jet fighters, ammunition etc, the prices of these rise called quasi-rent.The surplus over & above the minimum supply in the short run is called quasi-rent.

Theories on Interest:-Intrest is the price for using the services of capital.The various theories to determine the interest are:-

1.Classical Theory of Interest:-This theory was given by classical economists Marshall,Pigou,Tossig & others.According to this theory rate of interest is determined at at a point where real saving equals the real investment.So it also known as the real or S-I theory.

Saving:-Saving means what is not consumed , but here saving is real,i.e.assets, property, tools machinery etc. Thus saving is the supply of capital & is direct function of the rate of interest(ROI) ,i.e.

S=f(r) where S is supply of capital, f is function & r israte of interest.Hence supply curve SS is upward sloping as shown in the figure 4.6(a) below:

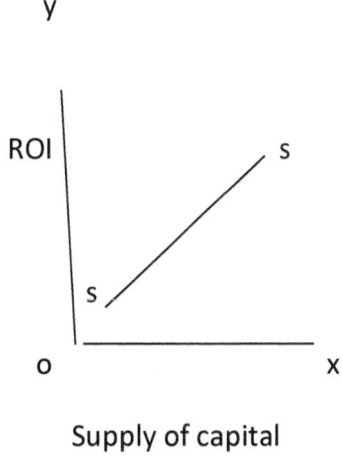

Supply of capital

Fig.4.6(a) Supply of Capital

Demand for capital or Investment(I):-Capital has marginal productivity i.e. MP× Price of the product.The marginal productivity is the return on the capitalor investment. Thus investment demand will be more if capital is cheap & returns are high.As for using capital, investor pays interest, so demand for capital is negative function of the rate of interest,i.e.I=f(1/r), where I is investment or capital demand,r is rate of interest,hence investment curve II, slopes downward as shown in the figure 4.6(b):

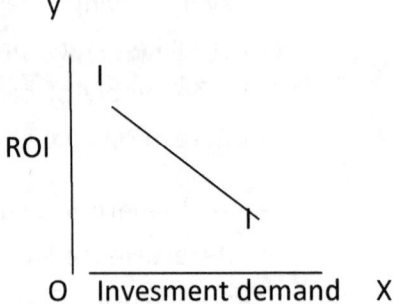

Fig.4.6(b) Demand for Capital

Equilibrium ROI:-The equilibrium rate of interest is found at a point where SS curve cuts the II curve as in the figure below:- In figure 4.6(c), E is the equilibrium point ,thus OR is the equilibrium ROI & OQ is the equilibrium quantity of capital..

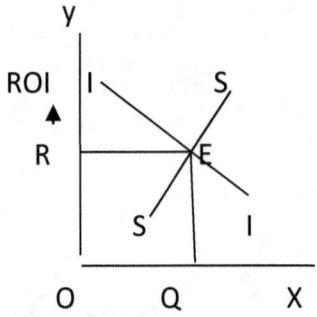

Fig.4.6(c) Equilibrium rate of interest

2.Loanable Fund Theory(LFT) OR Neo-Classical Theory:-:- This theory was prounded by a Swedish economist ,Knut Wicksell.In this theory both real & monetary sectors are mixed.

Theory:-According to this theory the equilibrium rate of interest is determinined at a point where the   demand for loanable fund equals the supply of loanable funds.

Explanation:-The theory can be explained as under:

1. Demand for loanable funds (Dlf):-The demand for loanable funds comes on account of:

a. Consumption demand or dissaving(DS):-Consumption means what is not saved, so it is called dissaving.As the funds are required for consumption but for funds there is price ,i.e. interest so law of demand applies ,i.e.$=f(1/r)$

b.Investment Demand(I):-It is required for the business purpose, to add the capital stock, it is real investment demand & is negative function of the rate of interest,i.e. $I=f(1/r)$.

c.Hoarding demand(H):-Hoarding means keeping idle cash & depends upon the rate of interest in the economy, if higher interest hoarding will be low & vice versa ,so $H=f(1/r)$.

Adding C,I& H we total demand for the loanable fund as in the figure 4.7(a) below:-

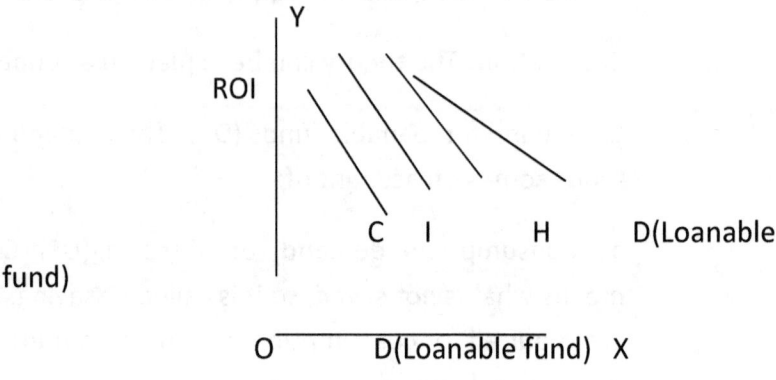

Fig.4.7(a) Demand for loanable fund

Supply of Loanable Funds:-The supply of loanable funds comes on account of;-

a. Savings(S):-Saving means what is not consumed, here it is real saving of capital & is a positive function of the rate of interest,i.e. S=f(r), where r is interest rate.

b.Bank Money(BM):-Bank money ,i.e. loan money is positive function of the rate of interest.

c.Disinvestment (DI):-It is the withdrawal of investment or capital depreciation & is a positive function of the rate of interest, i.e.=f(r).

d.Dishoarding (DH):-It means releasing idle cash held& is positive function of the rate of interest, i.e. S=f(r), where r is interest rate.

Adding all S,BM,DI,DH ,we get total supply of loanable fund for which the curve is positive as in the figure 4.7(b) below:

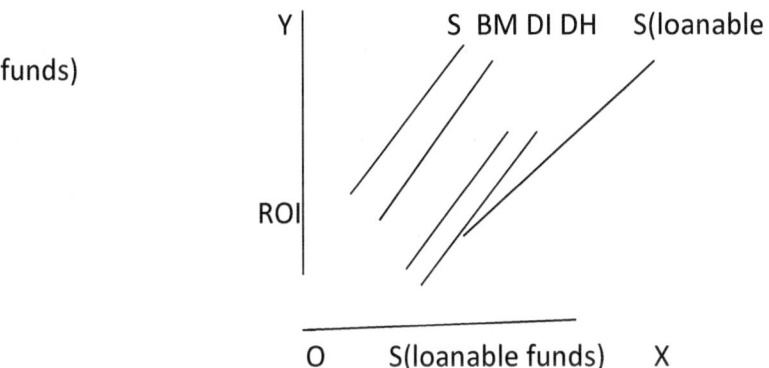

Fig.4.7(b) Supply of Loanable Fund

Equilibrium ROI:-The equilibrium rate of interest comes at a point where the supply curve of loanable funds cuts the demand curve as shown in the figure 4.7(c) below: In figure E is the equilibrium point where the S&D for loanable funds is equal, so OR is the equilibrium rate of interest & OQ is the equilibrium quantity of funds.

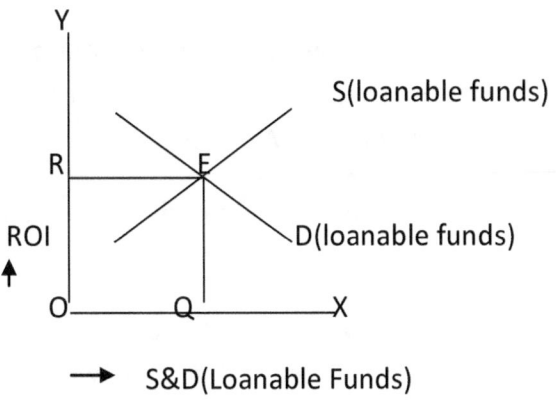

Fig.4.7(c) Equilibrium Point

Criticism:-

- 1.The theory mixes the real & monetary sectors which is not possible.
- 2.The theory does not talk of income level without which saving cannot be known, hence rate of interest cannot be determined.
- 3.Theory fails to determine the equilibrium ROI in reality.

...............======...............

3. Keynesian Liquidity Preference Theory:-The theory was given by Sir J.M.Keynes in 1936, is known as monetary theory or LM theory

because it is based on demand for money & supply of money.

Theory:-According to this theory rate of interest is determined at a point where demand for money (Lp) is equal to supply of money(M1).The demand for money is called liquidity preference, i.e. desire for cash. Money is liquid in nature as it flows like water.

Demand for money (Lp):-According to Keynes demand for money has following three motives:-

1. Transaction Demand(Mt):-The transaction purpose includes day today needs, by consumers ,producers & is functction of current income, as income increases ,transaction demand also increases .

.

2.Precautionary Demand(Mp):-Precautionary demand arises on account of future contingencies as health care, child education, old age etc.It is also function of the income level.

Thus Mt+Mp=M & M=f(Y), where Y is income level in the economy.

3. Speculative Demand(M2):-This type of demand is for speculative investment , i.e. investing in expectation to earn the profits in future. It is the negative function of the rate of interest, i.e.

M2=f(1/r), where r is the interest rate.

So total money demand, Md=M1+M2.As the increase in income causes increase in the M1,so interest rate rises, thus specucalative demand(M2) falls causing ,Md to fall .Thus Md is a negative function of the rate of interest,i.e. Md=f(1/r) & Md curve known as liquidity preference curve(LP) falls downward to right, but after a point becomes perfectly elastic ,the point is known as Liquidity Trap meaning below which liquidity cannot fall even if the rate of interest as shown in the figure below:-

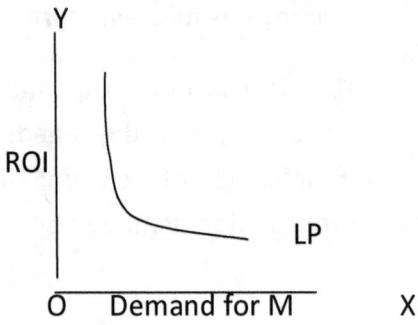

Fig.4.8(a) Demand for money

2.Money Supply(Ms):-According to Keynes,Ms is constant as it is supplied by the monetary authority, so money supply curve is parallel to oy-axis as shown in the figure 408(b).

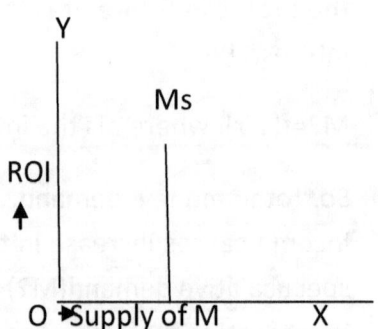

Fig.4.8(b) Supply of Money

Eqbm.:-The equilibrium rate of interest is determined is determined at a point where the money suplply equal to the money supply as shown in the figure 4.8(c) below:

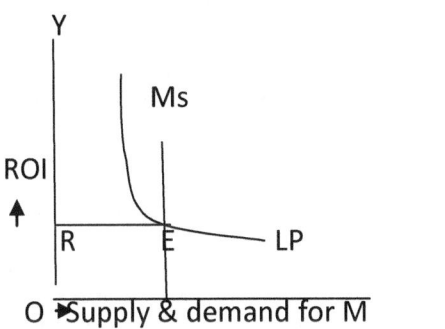

Fig.4.8(c):The Equilibrium point

In figure E is the equilibrium point where money demand cuts money supply ,thus OR is the equilibrium rate of interest.

Criticism:-

1.The theory ignores the real sector of the economy.

2.Has no answer for interest rate differentials.

3.Keeps only three motives of money demand.

Modern Theory of Interest Rate(IS-LM Model)(Hicks-Hansen Analysis ,1937):-According to the modern theory the rate of interest is determined at a point where IS curve cuts the LM curve .So the theory is known as IS-LM model.

IS curve:-As the income level in the economy rises, the savings also rise ,so the saving curve is positive sloping. The rising saving causes the rate of interest to fall & falling interest rate causes the investment to rise& vice –versa versa ,thus the IS-curve is downward to right as shown in the table & diagram below:-

Table:-IS schedule

Y	S	ROI	I	I=S,i.e.IS
100$	40$	5%	40$	40$
200$	50$	4%	50$	50$
300$	60$	3%	60$	60$
400$	70$	2%	70$	70$
500$	80$	1%	80$	80$

The table shows that as the income is rising ,the saving is also rising, so the rate of interest falls.The falling rate of interest causes the I to rise ,thus I=S.

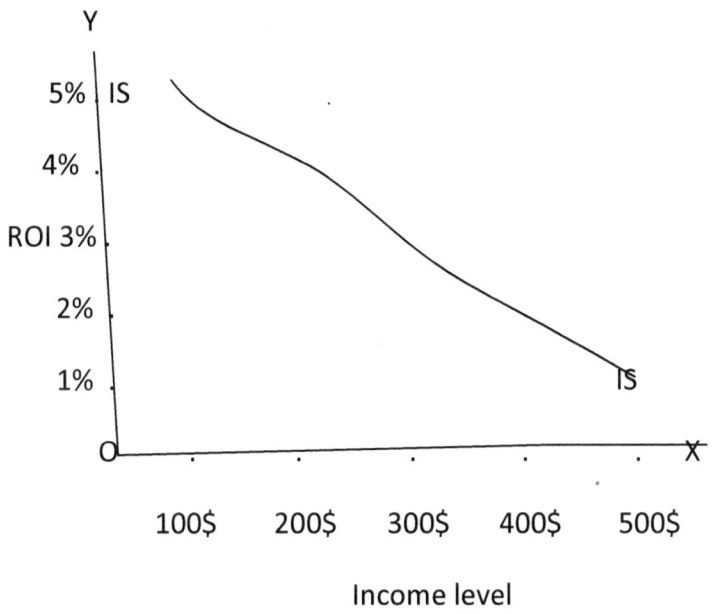

Fig.4.9(a) The IS-Curve

LM curve:-The LM curve stands for liquidity preference & money supply curve. As in the economy Ms =Md, so money is supplied by the monetary authority as per the money demand.LP is consisting of transaction ,precautionary ,M1& speculative demand,M2.M1 I function of income level, & has positive relation with the income level, but increasing M1 causes the ROI to fall, hence M2 to rise as shown in the table below:

Table:-LM schedule

Y	M1	ROI	M2	LP=Ms,i.e.LM
100$	10$	1%	50$	60$
200$	20$	2%	40$	60$
300$	30$	3%	30$	60$

400$	40$	4%	20$	60$
500$	50$	5%	10$	60$

The table shows that as the income is rising ,the M1 is also rising, so the rate of interest rises.The rising rate of interest causes the M2 to fall ,thus Md=Ms.

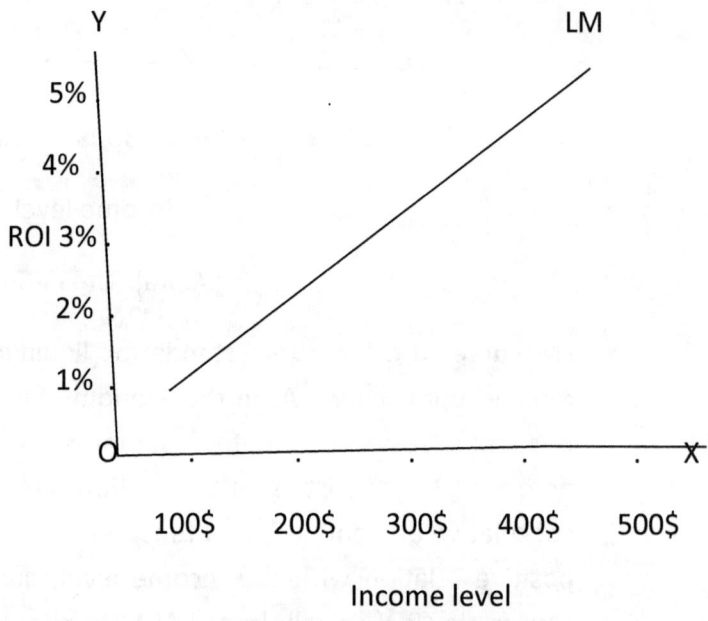

Fig.4.9(b):The LM-Curve

Equilibrium ROI:-Equilibrium ROI is determined at a point where IS curve cuts the LM curve as shown in the figure 4.9(c) below:-

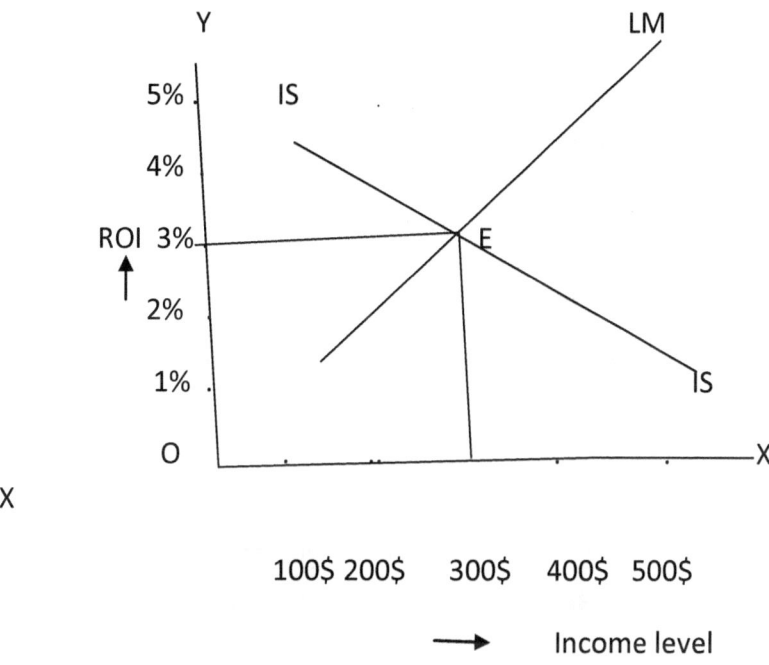

Fig.4.9(c):The Equilibrium Point

In figure ,E is the equilibrium point where IS=LM=60$,thus 3% is the equilibrium ROI at income level 300$.

Theories of Profits:-

1. **Risk Theory**:-This theory was given by Prof. Hawley. According to this theory the profit is the reward for the risk taking.

Main points of the theory:-

1. Profit is the reward for the risk.

2. More the risk, more the profits.

3. No risk, no profits.

4. Risk is taken for the purpose of earning profits.

Criticism:-

1. Profit is to avoid the risk not to take risk.

2. Theory does not talk of monopoly profits.

3. Prof. Knight says all types of risk don`t bring profits.

4. Prof. Samuelson says risk comes for innovations.

2. **Uncertainty Theory:-**This theory was given by Prof. Knight. According to Prof. Knight the profits are for uncertainty bearing, i.e. non-insurable risks.

Main points of the theory:-

1. Risks are of two types:-

a. Insurance-Risks:-Insurance risks are the risks which can be insured such as fire, theft, accident etc.

b.Non-Insururable Risk(Uncertainty bearing):-Non-insurable risks are the risks which cannot be covered by insurance as govt. policy change, change demand, tastes preferences etc.Such risks are uncertain, so taking such risk is uncertainty bearing.

2. Profit is the reward for the uncertainty bearing.

2. More the uncertainty bearing, more the profits.

3. No uncertainty bearing, no profits.

4. Uncertainty bearing is taken for the purpose of earning profits.

Criticism:-

1. Profit is to avoid the risk not to take risk.

2. Theory does not talk of monopoly profits..

3. Prof. Samuelson says risk comes for innovations.

3. Innovation Theory:-This theory was given Prof. Samuelson.According to this theory profits are for innovation & innovations are new ideas, new products, new methods, new machines, and new set up in organization etc.

Main points:-

1. Profits are innovations:-Innovations include introducing new ideas, techniques, methods etc 2.Innovations bring profits.

3. Innovations are carried by innovators:-It is the innovator who brings the profits not the capitalist who finances the business.

4. Innovations are for:-The innovator innovates because he enjoys doing things, wants to conquer others & lay down his business empire. This all brings profit.

4. Innovations appear, disappear & reappear:-Innovations appear & when they become common & known to all firms, thus they disappear & finally they reappear again when new innovations are brought.

5. Profits are frictional:-The profits are temporary because as innovations appear , profits appear, when innovations disappear, profits disappear & reappear when innovation reappear.

6.No innovation ,no profits:-If there are no innovations , there would be no profits.

Criticism:-

1.The theory considers one factor ,i.e. profits only.

2.The theory ignore risk as one of the factor in business.

3.Theory does not talk of monopoly profits.

4.Theory gives role of innovation to the innovator but at present innovation is the result of joint stock companies.

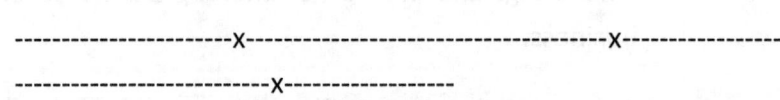

----------------------x---------------------------------x-----------------
--------------------------x-------------------

Unit **V**   **Welfare Economics**

Tits-bits:

Social Welfare: It means happiness of the society, i.e. economic & social well being.

Value judgements: To see the good & bad of the policy or decisions.

Classical welfare concept: It indicates social welfare is the sum of the welfare of all individuals in the society.

Paretian Social welfare: According to Sir Pareto if one is given benefit & none is harmed, it is social welfare or social improvement.

Compensation principle: According to this principal the gainer of the policy should compensate the looser of the policy.

Theory of the First best: According to this theory the economy should achieve the point of bliss which ensures economy & equity at the same time.

Theory of the second best: According to this theory if 1st best is not possible, then second best should be achieved.

Welfare Economics:

Welfare means happiness of the society & happiness is possible when the needed goods & services are available to the society at all times at affordable prices. The branch of economics which deals with welfare aspects, ethics & norms, value judgments, i.e. good & bad of the policies etc is known as the welfare economics.

Concepts:-

1. **Classical concept**:-According to classical social welfare is sum of individual welfare, assuming cardinal utility i.e.

$W = f(U1+U2+U3+....+Un)$, where W is social welfare, $U1, U2, U3$ are welfare levels of 1st, 2nd, 3rd & so on Un for no. of individuals.

2.**Pareto;-**Sir Pareto, Italian Economist, says it better to have the welfare of at least one individual, without harming any individual. Pareto calls it social welfare when some individuals are made better , providing none is made worse off on the basis of ordinal utility.

2. **Kaldor-Hicks**:-Social welfare is possible when the losers of the policy are compensated by the gainers of the policy known as compensation principle.

3. **Bergson-Samuelson**:-According to them social welfare is ordinal concept & is function of welfare of all individuals of the society, i.e.

$W=f(W1,W2,W3,....,Wn)$ where W is social welfare & w1,w2,w3,Wn are the welfare levels of 1st, 2nd & so on no. of individuals, f is function is maximum when 1st best is achieved, i.e. where social production equals the social consumption ensuring equity & efficiency.

Role of value judgments:-The value judgments indicate judging values & norms, ethics & behavior, good & bad, positive & negative aspects. In welfare economics value judgments is the normative part & analysis the good & bad of the policy & thus signals the necessary changes in the decision making of the authorities. Thus value judgments have important role as:

1. Policy & decision making:-The policy & decision effecting the social & economic development.

2. Budgeting:-The income, expenditure policies of the government, how to spend for the poor & tax the rich.

3. Welfare planning & programming:-That starting welfare programmes for upliftment of the low income groups of the population.

4. Direct social actions & practices:-Direct measure as tax concessions, subsidies, guidelines to creditors regard to the poor, preferential treatments to the disadvantaged groups.

Paretian Welfare Economics & Condition:-

Concept of Pareto Optimum:-According to Pareto, welfare is maximized when at least one person is made better off & none is made worse off. That if A & B are two individual earning Rs200/day at work, but due to some policy change say road provision to A`s village, A`s earns now Rs400 & B earns the same. For Pareto this situation is welfare known as Paretian optimum or efficiency.

Explanation:-Paretian concept can be explained with the help of Prof Samuelson`s production possibility curve as shown in figure:

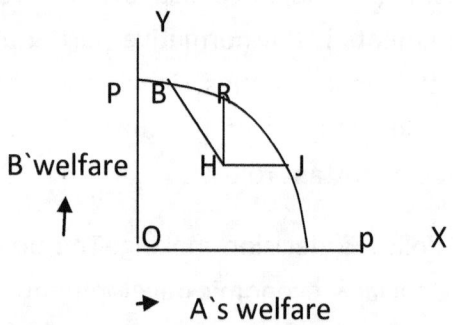

In figure:-

- Along ox-axis we have taken welfare of A & along oy-axis welfare of B.
- PP is the production possibility curve at which all points are efficient or optimum.
- H is the initial distribution of welfare.
- Jump from H to R improves the welfare of B, but of A remains the same. Same is for jump from H to J, where welfare of A increases. This explains the Pareto`s Optimum.
- However Pareto fails to answer where one is better off & 2nd is worse off as jump from H to B, where B is

better off but A is looser because now A is consuming less than H, his previous level.

Conditions:-1ˢᵗ order or marginal condition:-These conditions have been derived be Hicks & Lerner & are based on following assumptions.

- Utility is ordinal in nature.
- Consumers & producers are rational in nature.
- Every consumer buys some goods.
- Production function & technology given & constant for the firm.
- Goods are perfectly divisible & factors are perfectly mobile.
- Pareto keeps welfare economics free from value judgments & interpersonal comparison of utility.

1. Efficiency in consumption:-It means MRSxy for all consumers consuming two goods x & y should be same as explained with Edgeworth Box diagram.

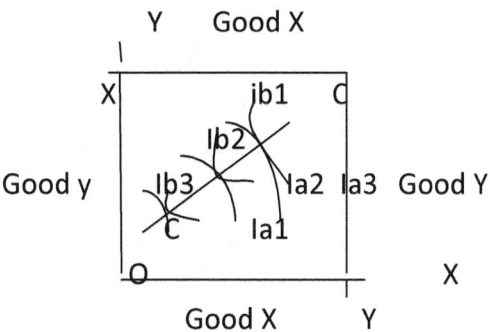

2. Efficiency in production:-It means $MRTS_{LK}$ should be same for all the firms using lab. & capital.

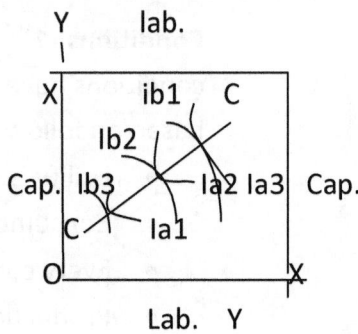

3. Efficiency in Factor- product mix:-It means MP of the factor say labour should be same for all the firms using labour.

4. Efficiency in product substitution:-It means MRTxy for individual=MRTxy for community.

5. Efficiency in specialization:-It means MRTxy should be same for all the firms.

6. Efficiency in Allocation of factor time:-It means MRSwork &leisure for income = MRSwork hrs. & product.

7. Efficiency in allocation of assets:-It means MRS between money assets at any time should same for any two individuals or any two firms.

2nd **order condition**:-All indifference curves are convex to the origin & all production possibility curves are concave to the origin.

Total order condition:-Once welfare attained with reallocation it should not be possible to make one better off without making any one worse off.

Kaldor-Hicks Compensation Principal:-According to Kaldor-Hicks welfare criteria developed in 1939-40, the looser of the policy should be compensated by the gainer of the policy, as the gainer still remains better off. So Kaldor-Hicks answer the Paretian failure where some become better off & others worse off.

Explanation:-Kaldor-Hicks principal can be explained with the help of Prof Samuelson`s production possibility curve as shown in figure:

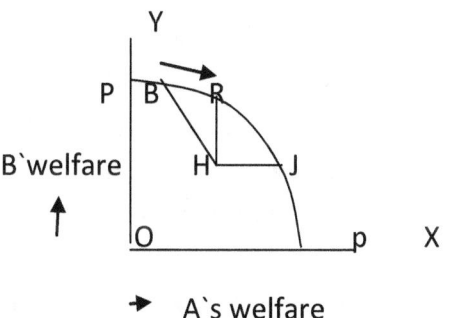

In figure :-Along ox-axis we have taken welfare of A & along oy-axis welfare of B.

- PP is the production possibility curve at which all points are efficient or optimum.
- H is the initial distribution of welfare.

- Jump from H to R improves the welfare of B, but of A remains the same. Same is for jump from H to J, where welfare of A increases. This explains the Pareto`s Optimum.
- However Pareto fails to answer where one is better off & 2nd is worse off as jump from H to B, where B is better off but A is looser because now A is consuming less than H, his previous level.
- So A should be compensated by B for policy gains as shown by arrow, & still B will be in a better position.

Scitovsky, a Hungarian economist in 1941, in his paper "A note on welfare propositions in Economics" developed criterion as Kaldor-Hicks test may fail & thus inconsistent when two production possibility curves intersect each other known **as Scitovsky paradox** as shown in the figure below: In figure, F on CIC2 is better than H on CIC1, at F,K-H passes but at the same time G on CIC1 is better than N on CIC2, because K-H again passes .This is contradictory as F is superior to G & G is superior to F.

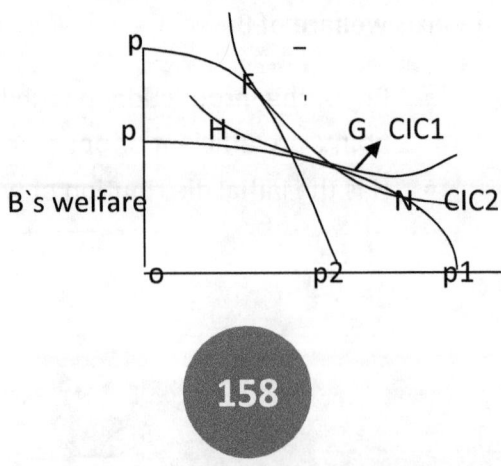

A`s welfare

Resolving the paradox:- To resolve the paradox the two possibility curves should not intersect each other as shown below:-As in figure at F,B gains & A is looser but B can move towards R, K-H criteria is satisfied but reversal is not possible

.

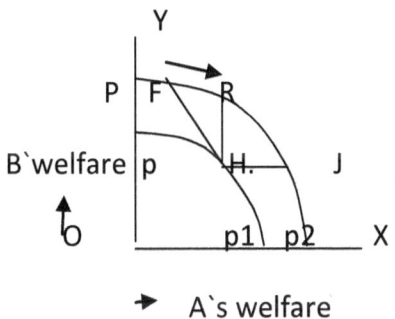

A`s welfare

Criticism:-

1.K-H principal does not call for actual compensation.

2. The gainers or losers may refuse & disagree for compensation.

3. Accoding to Prof Boumol not free from value judgments & inter-personal comparison of utility.

4. According to Prof. Boumol, Little & Arrow this principle is social desirability not social welfare.

5. Keeps production as primary basis of social welfare & distribution as secondary, but the fact is that production can not be separated from distribution.

Bergson-Samuelson New Social welfare Function:-The New Social Welfare Function (SWF) has been developed in 1938 by Bergson. According to this concept social welfare is maximum when 1st best is achieved with equity & efficiency. This is known as the point of Bliss for the economy. This is achieved when social indifference curve is tangent to the social production possibility curve.

Assumptions:-

1. The SWF is individualistic in nature.

2. Value judgments have to be taken from outside.

3. It is based on ordinal utility.

Explanation:-The SWF can be explained with the help of

a. Social indifference map

b.Social production possibility curve

a. **Social indifference map:-**As the social welfare is function of individual wefares ,i.e.

SW=f(W1,W2,W3,..........,Wn),so the set of various individual social welfare curves is known as social indifference map as shown below in the figure:-

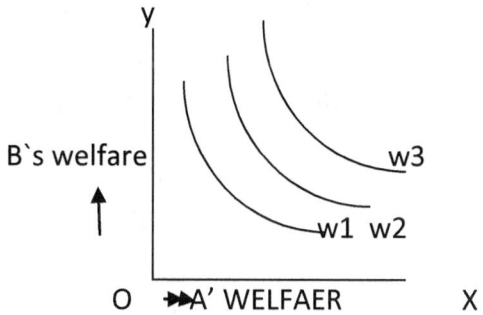

Fig. Social Indifference Map

b.**Social production possibility curve**:-The production possibility curve for the economy can be shown as under in the figure:-

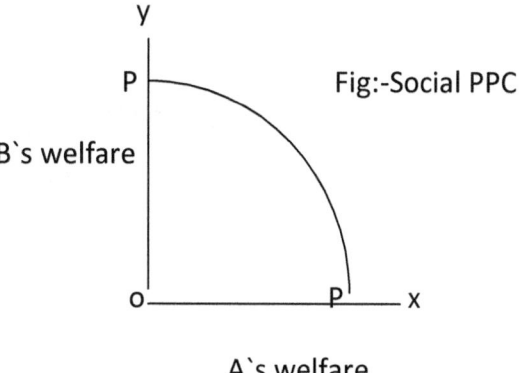

A`s welfare

The point of Bliss or social constraint:- For this point we have to bring the social indifference map & the social PPC together as shown below in the figure:-In figure:-

- Along ox-axis we have taken A`s welfare & along oy-axis welfare of B.
- PP is the social production possibility curve.
- W1, W2,W3,Wn are the the welfare levels of individuals in the society.
- E is the point of bliss where W2 is tangent to the social production possibility curve PP.The point E shows both equity as it shows equal distribution & efficiency as it operates on PPC.
- R & T can not be points of bliss because the are efficient but not equitable.More over they are on W1 which is lower level.
- W3 is not within the reach of the economy

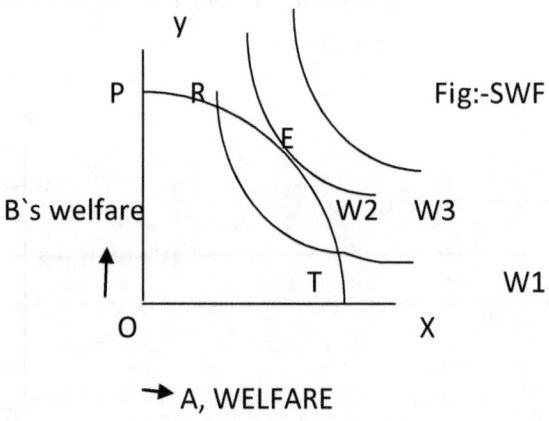

Fig:-SWF

....#...............................#....................

Refrences:-

Books:

1.Ahuja,H.L,Microeconomic Theory

2.Jhingan,M.L,Advanced Economic Theory

3.Bergin,James,Microeconomic Theory A Concise Course

4.Laidler,David,Introduction to Microeconomics

5. Chopra,P.N,Principles of Microeconomics

6.Dhingra,I.C,Microeconomic Theory

7.Jain,T.R,Introductory Micro & Macroecomics

E-Books:

8.Rode, Sanjay,Modern Microeconomics

9.Dilts,A.David,Introduction to Microeconomics

10.Ahlersten ,Krister,Essentials of Microeconomics

www.ingramcontent.com/pod-product-compliance
Lightning Source LLC
Chambersburg PA
CBHW051916170526
45168CB00001B/410